Bookmarks
London, Chicago and Melbourne

Peter Alexander

Racism, resistance and revolution

Racism, resistance and revolution
by Peter Alexander

Published July 1987
Bookmarks, 265 Seven Sisters Road, London N4 2DE, England
Bookmarks, PO Box 16085, Chicago, Illinois 60616, USA
Bookmarks, GPO Box 1473N, Melbourne 3001, Australia
Copyright: Bookmarks and Peter Alexander

ISBN 0 906224 36 5

Printed by Cox and Wyman Limited, Reading, England
Typeset by Gerry Norris
Cover design by Roger Huddle

BOOKMARKS is linked to an international grouping of socialist
organisations:

AUSTRALIA: **International Socialists**, GPO Box 1473N, Melbourne 3001.
BELGIUM: **Socialisme International**, 9 rue Marexhe, 4400 Herstal, Liege.
BRITAIN: **Socialist Workers Party**, PO Box 82, London E3.
CANADA: **International Socialists**, PO Box 339, Station E, Toronto, Ontario.
DENMARK: **Internationale Socialister**, Morten Borupsgade 18, kld, 8000
Arhus C.
FRANCE: **Socialisme International** (correpondence to Yves Coleman, BP407,
Paris Cedex 05).
IRELAND: **Socialist Workers Movement**, PO Box 1648, Dublin 8.
NORWAY: **Internasjonale Sosialister**, Postboks 5370, Majorstua, 0304 Oslo 3.
UNITED STATES: **International Socialist Organization**, PO Box 16085,
Chicago, Illinois 60616.
WEST GERMANY: **Sozialistische Arbeiter Gruppe**, Wolfgangstrasse 81, 6000
Frankfurt 1.

This book is published with the aid of the **Bookmarks Publishing Co-operative**. Many socialists have a few savings put aside, probably in a bank or savings bank. While it's there, this money is being loaned by the bank to some business or other to further the aims of capitalism. We believe it is better to loan to a socialist venture to further the struggle for socialism. That's how the co-operative works: in return for a loan, repayable at a month's notice, members receive free copies of books published by Bookmarks. The co-operative currently has about 160 members, from as far apart as London and Melbourne, Oslo and Seattle.

Like to know more? Write to the **Bookmarks Publishing Co-operative**, 265 Seven Sisters Road, Finsbury Park, London N4 2DE, England.

Contents

Dedication

For Moses Mayekiso, general secretary of the National Union of Metal Workers of South Africa, currently detained in an apartheid gaol, charged with treason. His bravery, humility and determined commitment to class struggle should be an inspiration to all opponents of racism.

ERRATUM: Page 148, line 28, should read: 'In Britain, Haringey Council has appointed a race advisory officer who is openly anti-gay.'

Introduction

WE LIVE in a racist society. In Britain and other Western countries black people are subject to various forms of racial oppression. In general they are paid lower wages, suffer more unpleasant working conditions, and live in worse housing than white people. The state itself works against them, subjecting Blacks to persecution and harassment at the hands of racist police and immigration officers. Black people's experience, their histories and cultures, are generally denied adequate expression in the mass media and the education system.

The problem which this book addresses is how we are to understand the nature of racism in order the better to struggle against it. The dominant view of racism makes certain assumptions which rarely rise to the level of theory It assumes that racism is a matter of irrational and repugnant attitudes, which certain white people hold about individuals with dark-coloured skins, and which may lead to violent and evil actions. Awareness and education are held to be the key to combatting these ideas, with legislation the way to prevent the practice of racism. An alternative view is that racism is endemic in 'white society'. In this case the solution offered is that black people must organise themselves separately from Whites in order to defend themselves and protect their interests.

Both these views are inadequate. Neither explains the origins of racism. Neither shows why racism varies, both in quality and degree, from one period of history to another and one society to another. Neither explains why some Whites are racist while others are actively anti-racist. Neither strategy has solved the problem of racism.

Racism can be properly understood only from a Marxist

perspective, which treats it as an historically specific, materially caused phenomenon. Racism is not, as is widely assumed, a universal feature of all societies. In the sense of discrimination against a group on the grounds of some imputed inherited characteristic, such as colour, racism is a product of capitalism. It grew out of early capitalism's thirst for slaves for the plantations of the New World, was consolidated in order to justify Western domination of the rest of the world, and flourishes today as a means of dividing the working class between insiders and outsiders, 'natives' and immigrants.

The first half of the book deals with the nature of racism. Chapter 1 provides a historical and materialist explanation of the origins and development of racism. Chapter 2 deals with the specific issue of immigration, and shows how in Britain both Labour and Tory governments have capitulated to racist pressures. Chapter 3 analyses racism in Britain today.

Understanding racism as a product of capitalism is essential to developing an adequate strategy for fighting it. In this century black people have been drawn towards two ways of fighting racism. The first is black nationalism, which claims that black people can achieve their liberation by organising separately. Chapters 4 and 5 examine the experience of this movement, especially in the United States, and shows how it failed because its leaders refused to seek unity with white workers in a struggle against the common enemy, capital. This failure has drawn black activists towards a second strategy, that of winning reforms from the system through electoral pressure. Jesse Jackson represents this approach in the US, the Labour Party Black Sections in Britain. Chapter 6 shows that the Labour Party's rotten record of capitulation to racism is a consequence of its commitment merely to reform the system, which leads Labour governments to prop up the existing order, racism and all. Labour's reformism means that it cannot be an instrument for black liberation.

The conclusion, drawn in Chapter 7, is that black people can free themselves only as part of the broader working-class struggle for socialism. White workers have no interest in preserving racial oppression, which divides and weakens their class. A revolutionary socialist party embracing both Blacks and Whites is essential to forging the united and self-conscious working class which, in overthrowing capitalism, must also destroy racism.

This book is written as part of the struggle to build such a party.

It is not a dry academic study, but a Marxist analysis and polemic which seeks to win people, both black and white, to revolutionary socialism. If it succeeds in this aim it will have been justified.

I am indebted to Alex Callinicos and Peter Marsden for the numerous improvements which they have made to this book; to Tony Cliff, Lindsey German, Chris Harman and Sheila McGregor, who contributed a large number of valuable criticisms; and to my father, John Alexander, for correcting various drafts and providing the index. I am grateful to many comrades for their advice and encouragement, but particularly Caroline O'Reilly, without whose support and affection this book would not have been possible.
Peter Alexander

Peter Alexander is a member of the Socialist Workers Party. He was National Organiser of the Anti Nazi League, and is Treasurer of the Campaign Against Racist Laws.

Chapter 1:
The Roots of Racism

RACISM IS commonly assumed to be as old as human society itself. People, so the argument goes, have always discriminated and oppressed each other — it's just human nature. This assumption is one form of the idea that human beings are naturally greedy, violent and selfish, which is, of course, also the most widespread argument used by those who say socialism would not work.

Belief in the universality of racism doesn't stand up to historical examination. Racism is a particular form of oppression: discrimination against people on the grounds that some inherited characteristic which is attributed to them, for example colour, makes them inferior to their oppressors. Class societies before capitalism were able, on the whole, to do without this form of oppression.

The societies of classical antiquity — ancient Greece and Rome — were brutal in the extreme, based as they were on the exploitation of slave labour. But, as C L R James put it:

> ... historically it is pretty well proved now that the ancient Greeks and the Romans knew nothing about race. They had another standard — civilised and barbarian — and you could have a white skin and be a barbarian and you could be black and civilised.[1]

People were enslaved usually as a result of conquest. Since white people were conquered as well as Blacks, Whites were also enslaved. Indeed, the majority of slaves were white.[2] For instance, Cicero took a dim view of slaves from Britain, who were considered to be excessively stupid.[3] In these circumstances racism would have been useless as a justification for slavery.

This is not to say that the ancients knew nothing of oppression — they did — but they justified it in terms of culture, not race. A barbarian could become civilised by the process of, for instance, learning the Greek language and obtaining a Greek education. By these means Blacks were able to rise to positions of great importance in the ancient Greek and Roman world.[4]

The ancients encountered Blacks as able fighters to be treated with respect and not disdain. Alexander the Great's march of conquest was turned back by dark-skinned people in the Indian sub-continent. In North Africa the Greeks and the Romans met substantial black opposition.

Frank M Snowden, in his book **Before Color Prejudice**, considered a variety of evidence. He concluded that: 'The ancients did accept the institution of slavery as a fact of life; they made ethnocentric judgements of other societies; they had narcissistic canons of physical beauty ... Yet nothing comparable to the virulent color prejudice of modern time existed in the ancient world'. He added that: 'This is the view of most scholars who have examined the evidence ...'[5]

This does not mean, of course, that pre-capitalist societies were enlightened. Racism, when it began to develop with the rise of capitalism, contained elements of earlier prejudices. Thus, in the largely self-sufficient village typical of feudalism, someone from another village was defined as a 'foreigner'. In time, as market relationships penetrated these hitherto closed feudal worlds, 'foreigner' began to be applied to people from further afield.

The parochial prejudices of pre-capitalist societies were, however, different from racism in two important respects. First, they helped maintain a distinction between those who belong (to the village and the lord) and outsiders *in general*. They weren't aimed at *particular* minorities. Secondly, racism supposes a relationship of superior to inferior. Prejudice assumes an attitude to something which is merely different, although possibly unusual or even incomprehensible.

Racism itself took shape in the course of the development of capitalism. As we shall see, it has assumed three successive forms, the *racism of slavery*, the *racism of empire*, and *anti-immigrant racism*.

SLAVERY AND THE ORIGINS OF RACISM

The first clear evidence of racism occurs at the end of the sixteenth century.

In 1555 a group of black Africans had arrived in London. This was eight years before John Hawkins initiated Britain's involvement in the slave trade. Nevertheless, from the beginning, their status seems to have been that of slaves. At first they were welcomed. Because of their rarity, exotic nature and curiosity value, black slaves began to figure prominently as servants in more and more upper class households.[6]

More than any other single person, Queen Elizabeth I was responsible for the early settlement of black people in England. Not only did she encourage the growing English involvement in the trade in black slaves, she also employed Africans at court.[7] But, for our rulers, hypocrisy has always been close at hand, and in 1596 she tried to have the Africans deported. She had an open letter distributed which declared:

> Her Majesty understanding that several blackamoors have lately been brought into this realm, of which kind of people there are already too many here ... her Majesty's pleasure therefore is that those kind of people should be expelled from the land ...[8]

The 1590s saw a series of bad harvests and other economic problems, and as a consequence it was a period of social crisis. Elizabeth argued that there were already enough people in Britain (about four million) without the Blacks and they were taking food out of her subjects' mouths.[9] The similarity between this and the scapegoating of Blacks today, in the reign of Elizabeth II, is obvious. Although it was argued that most of the 'Blackamoors' were 'infidels', they were all to be expelled whatever their religion. The attack was on Blacks as a group, and thus racist.

There is other evidence of racism in this period. The historian James Walvin provides a number of examples of racism in the writings of William Shakespeare. For example: 'Such Ethiope words, blacker in their effect than in their countenance' (*Much Ado About Nothing* V iv). However, he concludes:

> While Shakespeare played on his contemporaries' jaundiced reactions to black humanity, there is proof, scattered throughout his works, that personally he did not approve of, or believe in, the common mythology about Africans.[10]

The material basis for these new racist ideas — in economic crisis — was strengthened by the growth of the trans-Atlantic slave trade and by the increasing use of black slaves in the American colonies.

According to C L R James:

> ... the conception of dividing people by race begins with the slave trade.
> This thing [the slave trade] was so shocking, so opposed to all the
> conceptions of society which religion and philosophers had ... that the
> only justification by which humanity could face it was to divide people
> into races and decide that the Africans were an inferior race.[11]

Slavery in the West Indies and the Americas differed radically
from its ancient predecessor. Slavery in classical times served to
support the leisured life-style of a landed ruling class. Slavery as it
developed after the European conquest of the New World, on the
other hand, was an essential element in what Marx called 'the
primitive accumulation of capital', the concentration of wealth in the
hands of a new capitalist class oriented on production for profit. It
was part of the creation of a new world system based on the restless
search for profit. Slavery in the new world was more rapacious than
in the ancient world. As Marx says: ' ... overworking of the negro and
sometimes the using up of his life in seven years of labour became a
factor in a calculated and calculating system.'[12]

It was in this environment that racism was formed, as an attempt
to justify the most appalling and inhuman treatment of black people
in the slave trade and the plantation slavery of the New World — in
the service of the greatest accumulations of material wealth the world
had until then seen. This view of the origin of racism is supported by
Peter Fryer, author of an excellent history of black people in Britain,
Staying Power. Fryer considers the account of Morgan Godwyn's **The
Negro's and Indians Advocate**, published in 1680, and concludes:

> First of all, racist ideology was created by the planters and slave-
> merchants out of 'avarice'. Second, it was spread at first in whispers,
> furtively. Third, by 1680 it had become respectable enough — had
> gained enough 'strength and reputation' — for its propagators in
> England to have come into the open (though not yet in print). Fourth,
> opponents of racism were as yet few and uninfluential. And lastly, one
> of racism's functions was to justify the planters and merchants in their
> own eyes as well as the eyes of the rest of society.[13]

So, by the end of the seventeenth century, racism, as an ideology,
was still in the process of being formed. Before the end of the next
century, however, it had become an established, systematic and
conscious justification for the most degrading forms of slavery. By
1771, even the philosopher David Hume was lending credibility to the

cause of racism:

> I am apt to suspect the Negroes ... to be naturally inferior to the Whites ... There never was a civilised nation of any other complexion than white, or even any individual eminent in either action, or speculation. No ingenious manufacturers among them, no arts, no sciences. There are Negro slaves dispersed all over Europe, of which none ever discovered any symptoms of ingenuity.[14]

Christianity and slavery

In common with other peoples of the ancient world, the early Christians do not appear to have been affected by racism.[15] There is a hint of prejudice in the famous line from the *Song of Solomon:* 'I am black, but comely'. However, this is a seventeenth century invention of the King James Bible, for the literal translation from the original Hebrew is 'I am black *and* comely'.[16] At the same time the early Christians tolerated and in some cases justified slavery, which was regarded as part of the natural order. This has led the Marxist historian G E M de Ste Croix to comment:

> Whatever the theologian may think of Christianity's claim to set free the soul of the slave, the historian cannot deny that it helped to rivet the shackles rather more firmly to his feet.[17]

However, certainly by the fifteenth century the enslavement of Christians was regarded as abhorrent. This arose partly from the general decline of slavery in Europe, partly — perhaps — from the need to galvanise the support of Christian peoples for the wars of the Crusaders to capture valuable trading routes and territories from the Islamic powers. When the Portuguese engaged in exploration and overseas conquest they attracted the support of the Pope on the basis that they would recapture Christians who had been enslaved. Such zeal did not prevent the Portuguese and Spaniards from retaining some black people as slaves. This they justified on the grounds that the 'natives' were unbelievers, which in turn led them to a dilemma.

As good Christians they had a responsibility to attempt to convert the 'natives', and for this reason missionaries accompanied every ship. But if the missionaries were successful it would be impossible for slavery to flourish. For the Spaniards the main problem was whether or not it was proper to subjugate the South American Indians before converting them.[18] This was the subject of a major theological debate sponsored by the Emperor Charles V and held in Vallodalid in 1550.

The issue was never formally resolved, but one of the major disputants, Juan Gines de Sepulveda, articulated a new, proto-racist line: that on account of the Indians' nature, and because of the gravity of the sins which they had committed, they were obliged to serve persons having a more refined nature ... such as the Spaniards.

In practice, the Portuguese and Spaniards found ways of combining their Christian ethics with their material concern to subjugate and enslave the Indians. In the process their justifications became increasingly racist.

Slavery and the English

The English had fewer compunctions about enslaving Africans and were more willing to develop the ideology most appropriate to this. A number of factors gave rise to slavery being associated with black skins.

There had been white slaves in England, but by the sixteenth century they were virtually non-existent. In common with other settlers in the New World, the English did not at first make use of African slaves. Native Indians were enslaved. Later, attempts were made to use 'unfree' white labour. This proved unsuccessful because it was impossible to find sufficient numbers of convicts and labourers willing to accept indentures binding them to their employers.[19] Wholesale enslavement of Whites (and therefore Christians) would have been socially, politically and economically unacceptable. Free labourers had the choice of moving on and setting up as independent farmers and consequently rejected the harsh conditions typical of the large estates suited to the production of sugar and cotton. The alternative was the exploitation of the plentiful and relatively cheap supplies of slaves available from Africa.

One of the most important studies of slavery was conducted by Eric Williams, who was a professor in the politics department of an American university before becoming the first prime minister of Trinidad and Tobago in 1961. In **Capitalism and Slavery** he argued that 'the origins of Negro slavery ... was economic, not racial; it had to do not with the colour of the labourer, but the cheapness of the labour.'[20]

The fact that these slaves were infidels, and not Christian, was used to help justify their enslavement. But racism, not religion, provided the main justification, for it had one major advantage.

Christianity could be acquired by the simple process of conversion. Ideologically, at least in the early days, there was a possibility that slaves could choose to be free by choosing to become Christian. Race was a different matter. You could not choose to become white. And because blackness was inherited, so was slavery. Racism not only provided a justification for enslaving certain people, it also justified the enslavement of their children and their children's children. This was something that slavery justified by religion or by culture had never achieved.

Fryer comments that 'the planters in the West Indies shared the widespread belief that if they let their black slaves be converted to Christianity and baptised this would mean setting them free,' but that 'the Church did its best to reassure the planters on that score.'[21] The planters nevertheless resisted the conversion of slaves. Godwyn describes their attitude:

> 'What, such as they?' they cried. 'What, those black dogs be made Christians?' And they demanded to know whether ministers of religion would start baptising horses.[22]

Racism's origin was thus as a justification of slavery. This became important with the growth of the trans-Atlantic slave trade in the seventeenth century. It became possible because all the slaves were black and all the masters white, and therefore developed as an ideology of white superiority. Had all the slaves been white, and all the masters black, the result would have been an ideology of black superiority.

IMPERIALISM AND THE DEVELOPMENT OF RACISM

In 1760, with the slave trade at its height, the twenty-three volume **Universal History**, published in London, expressed the following view of Africans:

> ... proud, lazy, treacherous, thievish, hot, and addicted to all kinds of lusts, and most ready to promote them in others, as pimps, panders, incestuous, brutish, and savage, cruel and revengeful, devourers of human flesh and quaffers of human blood, inconstant, base, treacherous, and cowardly ... It is hardly possible to find in any African any quality but what is of the bad kind: they are inhuman, drunkards, deceitful, extremely covetous, and perfidious to the highest degree ... If we look at those few manufactures and handicrafts that are

amongst them, we shall find them carried on with the same rude and tedious stupidity.[23]

The most common myths of the racist stereotype are all contained here. 'Africans' are portrayed as stupid, lazy, violent and promiscuous. One view particularly suited to the needs of slavery, that 'Africans' are sub-human, was developed by the eighteenth century historian, Edward Long, who wrote:

> When we reflect on ... their dissimilarity to the rest of mankind, must we not conclude, that they are a different species of the same genus? ... Nor do [orangutans] seem at all inferior in the intellectual faculties to many of the Negro race; with some of whom, it is credible that they have the most intimate connection and consanguinity. The amorous intercourse between them may be frequent ... and it is certain, that both races agree perfectly well in lasciviousness of disposition.[24]

These views are typical of the dominant attitude in Britain in the last part of the eighteenth century. But they did not go unchallenged. The movement for the abolition of the slave trade, in particular, 'one of the greatest propaganda movements of all time,'[25] held that the negro was 'A Man and a Brother'. In 1807 this movement secured the abolition of the British slave trade and in 1833 the abolition of slavery throughout the British Empire. The demands of the abolitionists met with the enthusiastic approval of the new industrial working class. One workers' meeting of the time resolved that, 'Wishing to be rid of the weight of oppression under which *we* groan, we are induced to compassionate those who groan also.'[26]

Further support for the abolition of slavery came from powerful industrial barons, particularly in centres such as Manchester, the 'Cotton Capital of the World', whose interests ran counter to those of the monopoly system — of which the slave trade was part. In the early days monopoly protected British interests; it ensured that goods and raw materials from the colonies had to be carried in British ships, to be sold in Britain in exchange for British manufactures. By the nineteenth century, however, with industry flourishing, it was becoming particularly burdensome, restricting access to new markets elsewhere. Eric Williams concluded:

> The commercial capitalism of the eighteenth century developed the wealth of Europe by means of slavery and monopoly. But in doing so it helped to create the industrial capitalism of the nineteenth century which turned round and destroyed the power of commercial

capitalism, slavery, and all its works.[27]

The abolitionists, in challenging slavery, had dented the credibility of racism. But it was a temporary and limited setback, not lasting beyond 1840. Rejuvenated and more powerful, racism no longer appeared as the hand-maiden of slavery but as the ideology of empire. This new *racism of empire* had three distinguishing characteristics. It was paternalistic, 'scientific', and nationalistic. It was to be the dominant form of racism for the next hundred years.

Paternalism

The following view of the typical African, presented by the colonial administrator, Lord Lugard, should be contrasted with that of the **Universal History** and Edward Long, recorded above:

> a happy, thriftless, excitable person, lacking in self-control, discipline, and foresight ... full of personal vanity, with little sense of veracity ... not naturally cruel, though his own insensibility to pain, and his disregard for life — whether his own or another's — cause him to appear callous to suffering ... In brief, the virtues and the defects of this race-type are those of attractive children ... It is extremely difficult ... to find educated African youths who are by character and temperament suited to posts in which they may rise to positions of high adminsitrative responsibility.[28]

Much of the old racist stereotype remains, but it is expressed in a more refined tone. So, for instance, 'deceitful' has become 'little sense of veracity', and 'brutish' has become 'appears callous to suffering'. A note of caution should be added in understanding this shift of *emphasis*: particularly when the army engaged in physically suppressing colonial revolts, the more 'robust' phraseology tended to reappear.[29] More substantial and significant is the way in which Africans appear not as something 'inhuman' or indeed sub-human and animal-like but as 'children'. For Lugard they were 'attractive children'; for others, whose experience was perhaps less pleasant, they were 'ungrateful children'.

The dominant view was summed up in Rudyard Kipling's poem, first published in 1889:

> Take up the White Man's burden —
> Send forth the best ye breed —
> Go, bind your sons to exile
> To serve your captives' need;

To wait, in heavy harness,
On fluttered folk and wild —
Your new-caught, sullen peoples,
Half devil and half child.

British colonialists thus cast themselves as father and mother, with a clear moral duty to take responsibility for the spiritual and material well-being of the children. Of course the children would need to be protected from other adults — and on occasion from themselves. This racist ideology worked wonders. Imperialism could be justified as philanthropy. Although divisions remained, many of those Christian people who had found slavery a little unsavoury could welcome imperialism with open arms. 'Child' might not be quite the same as 'Brother and a man', but then most of them had only meant a younger brother, much younger, only a little man, just a boy really!

Science

'Scientific' racism, which provided racism with a new intellectual credibility, had its origins in the scientific inquiries of the late eighteenth century. Linneaus, the Swedish naturalist who laid the basis for the modern classification of plants and animals, also, in 1758, distinguished four varieties of the human species. The confusion between biological and social characteristics was present from the beginning. This can be seen from the following descriptions of European man and African man:

> H. Europaei. Of fair complexion, sanguin temperament, and brawny form ... Of gentle manners, acute in judgement, of quick invention, and governed by fixed laws ...
>
> H. Afri. Of black complexion, phlegmatic temperament, and relaxed fibre ... Of crafty, indolent, and careless disposition, and governed in their actions by caprice.[30]

Linneaus was ahead of his time. 'Scientific' racism did not blossom until the nineteenth century, when anthropologists and others busied themselves collecting and measuring bones, particularly skulls. They started with an assumption of the superiority of European peoples and their 'scientific' enquiries always seemed to prove them correct. When Darwin's **Origins of Species** appeared in 1859, its theory of evolution was seized upon by the 'scientists' of race.

Darwin was not himself a racist. He demonstrated that Europeans and Africans belonged to the same species, which was related to the apes, thus disproving the old racist belief. This point was conveniently ignored by the 'Social Darwinists', headed by Herbert Spencer, the man who had invented the concept of 'survival of the fittest' eight years before **Origins of Species** had been published. The Social Darwinists believed that the white races were becoming dominant because they were 'naturally' superior, and that elimination of the inferior races would strengthen humanity. For example, Karl Pearson, a professor at London University, argued in 1901 that:

> History shows ... one way, and one way only, in which a high state of civilisation has been produced, namely, the struggle of race with race, and the survival of the physically and mentally fitter race ... This dependence of progress on the survival of the fitter race ... gives the struggle for existence its redeeming features.[31]

Thus 'science' could be used to justify, if necessary, not merely imperialist domination but oppression and even genocide. Race and religion joined hands in the service of empire, but race was dominant. In a world where religion no longer provided a satisfactory explanation of everything for everybody, race had a stamp of approval from the new god ... 'Science'. This racism of empire, scientific racism, helped to free Christianity from the inhibitions of the eighteenth century, so that in the nineteenth century it could blaze the trail for imperial expansion.

Nationalism

Race had one further advantage. Where religion tended to universalism, racism, especially the new racism, tended to the particular. It not only justified the domination of Whites over Blacks, it could be used to justify the domination of certain Christian Whites over other Christian Whites. Race could become nation, and nation could become race. The view that a nation was more than a collection of individuals, that it was a body of people related in blood, with a common history and common destiny was a powerful means of mobilising the masses in times of war. Winston Churchill understood this all too well with his talk of 'The Island Race'. As late as 1931, Sir Arthur Keith attempted to provide a scientific justification for the link between race and nation.

Give the inhabitants of any land a national spirit, let that land be preserved over many generations, and a race will certainly appear under the working of the law of evolution. A nation always represents an attempt to become a race; nation and race are but different degrees of the same evolutionary movement.[32]

According to the historian George Mosse, by the mid-nineteenth century many Englishmen had placed their nation within the Anglo-Saxon heritage.[33] At about the same time phrases like the 'English race' or 'British race' became widespread. The influential Scottish theorist Dr Robert Knox was then in his prime. Knox was not a chauvinist, and placed the Slavonic races highest because of their rationalism and ability for transcendental thought. But he praised the Saxons, not only as the strongest race, but also for their love of labour, love of order, punctuality in business, neatness and cleanliness — all good bourgeois virtues. The writings of Knox and other racial 'scientists' gave added weight to the chauvinism of politicians such as Disraeli, who in 1849 in the House of Commons, argued that: 'Race implies difference and difference implies superiority, and superiority leads to predominance.'[34]

Meanwhile, in Europe, one notorious racist, the Comte de Gobineau, was busy writing. He was different: a disaffected French nobleman who had been a cabinet secretary, in the wake of the 1848 revolution, he turned his back on France and dedicated his 'Essay on the Inequality of Races' to George of Hanover. He believed that the hope of the world was with the fair-haired Teutons, whom he called Aryan. Despite the fact that he could find no more than a handful of pure Aryans in Germany, and that Germany was no more Aryan than a number of other countries, Gobineau's theories were later taken up and embellished by German nationalists. These would include Adolf Hitler.

In Britain 'scientific' racism lost some of its appeal with the rise of Germany as a great rival. In the 1920s and 1930s the scientific basis of racism came under repeated attack particularly in America from cultural anthropologists such as Franz Boaz and Ruth Benedict. But the strongest blows to the racism of Empire came from a different direction.

The idea of black subject peoples as 'children' works well until the 'children' decide they want to be grown-ups. In India and then throughout Africa they fought to become free and independent adults. In the process the racism of empire was weakened as its material basis was undermined. Moreover, racism was taken to its logical conclusion in Nazi Germany. With the defeat of Hitler, the credibility of biological, 'scientific' racism was reduced to ashes.

One final point is worth making in passing. The period from about 1840 to 1918 was when racism reached its zenith. It was also the period when the number of black people in Britain reached a new low. Through the eighteenth century the number of Blacks was rising, reaching a peak of perhaps 20,000 and a distinct community existed at least in London. With the abolition of the slave trade the numbers tended to decline, perhaps to as low as 5,000 and the communities dispersed. This would seem to disprove the widely held view that the numbers of immigrants and the level of racism are closely related.

'WHITE NIGGERS'

At the same time that racism of empire was taking shape, racism in Britain was being strengthened by another force, opposition to the new immigrants from Ireland. It is no coincidence that this *anti-immigrant racism* should develop alongside the racism of empire. As industrial capitalism was rapidly expanding its interests overseas, at home the growth of factory production was drawing in a new generation.

Capitalism has always grown unevenly, and part of the process has involved the employment of new, 'foreign' workers. The so-called 'foreigners' have always provided the employers with the basis for encouraging a split within the workforce. The long boom of British capitalism after the second world war was to encourage the migration of West Indians and South Asians to Britain, and later this provided the basis for attacks on black 'foreigners'. A century and more earlier it was white 'foreigners', the Irish, who were being attacked. Despite the colour of their skin, the Irish suffered from racism. Marx compared them to the 'niggers' in America.[35]

The theories of 'scientific' racism so dominated the outlook of Victorian Britain that some doctors believed that the shape of the head and skull could be used as an indicator of racial type and intelligence. The Irish were held to be racially and therefore intellectually inferior, while the British, more particularly their upper classes, were thought to be superior.[36] Charles Kingsley, the novelist and clergyman, was among those who reflected this line of thinking. In 1860 he visited Sligo in the west of Ireland, and wrote:

> I am haunted by the human chimpanzees I saw along that hundred miles of horrible country ... To see white chimpanzees is dreadful; if they were black, one would not feel it so much.[37]

Irishmen had been coming to England for centuries, mostly to work as labourers, and since the seventeenth century there had been an Irish community in London. Many came initially to pay rent due to Anglo-Irish absentee landlords.[38] According to E P Thompson, the pace of migration accelerated during the counter-revolution which followed the defeat of the rebellion of the United Irishmen in 1798.[39] Two years later the Act of Union between England and Ireland added to the numbers of Irish migrant workers by helping to destroy industry in Ireland, such as linen and silk manufacture.

During the 1840s the Irish population in Britain virtually doubled, to reach almost 800,000.[40] The Irish were pulled by the industrial revolution, but pushed by famine. The misery of the Great Starvation, which claimed as many as one million lives, was started by the potato blight but *created* by the ravages of the landlord class. During the famine enough food was being produced in Ireland to feed the starving twice over. Corn was produced in abundance, but shipped off to England.[41] The landlords grew wealthy, while the poor emigrated or died. Marx described the situation:

> Begin with pauperising the inhabitants of a country, and when there is no more profit to be ground out of them, when they have grown a burden to the revenue, drive them away ...[42]

In England the Irish met some hostility from established workers. According to Thompson there were many riots, especially where English and Irish unskilled labour was in direct competition. He mentions pitched battles in the 1830s and 1840s which ended in fatal casualties.[43] Another historian, James Walvin, claims however that anti-Irish violence was uncommon.[44] Certainly people of Irish origin played a leading role in the greatest working-class movement of the nineteenth century, the Chartists.

It is certain, however, that there were widespread and deep-rooted antagonisms towards the Irish. The popular image of the Irishman was that of a dim-witted and violent drunk. This was a racist stereotype, and like many such stereotypes it contained a grain of truth — which is why it was believed. The most noticeable Irish immigrant was the 'navvy', working on the building of the canals and railways, probably living without his wife, and engaged in excessively strenuous and tedious labour. Drink provided some consolation, and violence often followed. Less distinctive was the immigrant Irish artisan, married to an English woman, with children who spoke English with a Lancashire accent. The latter were just as large in number, and rapidly becoming assimilated.

There were of course some real differences between the native English and immigrant Irish. Most but not all of the immigrants were Catholics and practised different customs. Most of the early immigrants also spoke a different language, Gaelic. But differences on their own do not lead to racism. This developed among working class people for one simple reason: the Irish were seen as competitors. They were correct in appreciating the problem, but mistaken about the enemy. A Birmingham employer gave the following evidence in 1836:

> The Irish labourers will work any time ... I consider them very valuable labourers, and we could not do without them. By treating them kindly, they will do anything for you ... an Englishman could not do the work they do. When you push them they have a willingness to oblige which the English have not; they would die under anything before they would be beat; they would go at hard work till they drop before a man should excel them.[45]

Doubtless the attitude of the Irish labourers was affected by the awful conditons of life in Ireland. Some employers were even more ruthless about the way in which they exploited this. One Manchester silk manufacturer is quoted as saying: 'The moment I have a turn-out [strike] and am fast for hands I send to Ireland for ten, fifteen or twenty families ...' And on at least two occasions, at Newton Heath and Preston, owners of mills brought over bands of immigrants from Ireland for the purpose of strike breaking.[46]

The view of the employers was contradictory. As individuals they might be sympathetic towards hard-working and low paid Irish immigrants. As a class they helped to maintain the anti-Irish stereotype, so valuable as a means of fuelling the divisions among workers. In this they were encouraged by a press whose chauvinism increased every time there was a need to justify the suppression of some stirring among the Irish. In this sense anti-Irish racism has always been intertwined with the politics of imperialism in Ireland.[47] This has also helped to shape Irish attitudes towards the English.

Karl Marx was probably the first writer to present a clear analysis of this anti-immigrant racism. In 1870 he wrote:

> And most important of all! Every industrial and commercial centre in England now possesses a working class *divided* into two *hostile* camps, English proletarians and Irish proletarians. The ordinary English worker hates the Irish worker as a competitor who lowers his standards of life. In relation to the Irish worker he feels himself a member of the *ruling* nation and so turns himself into a tool of the aristocrats and capitalists of his country *against Ireland*, thus strengthening their domination *over himself*.[48]

Marx adds that the English worker's attitude towards the Irish is 'much the same as that of the "poor Whites" to the "niggers" in the former slave states of the USA. The Irishman pays this attitude back with interest: he sees in the English worker at once the accomplice and the stupid tool of English rule in Ireland.' Marx then explains the attitude of the bourgeoisie and its impact on class struggle:

> This antagonism is artifically kept alive and intensified by the press, the pulpit, the comic papers, in short, by all means at the disposal of the ruling classes. This *antagonism* is the *secret of the impotence of the English working class,* despite its organisation. It is the secret by which the capitalist class maintains its power. And that class is fully aware of it.

RACISM AND ANTI-SEMITISM

Anti-semitism is often assumed to be a variant of racism. While it would be correct to regard modern anti-semites as racists, this analogy should not be extended back to cover all periods of history. Anti-semitism has not always been racial in character. This becomes clear from a reading of Abram Leon's invaluable analysis, **The Jewish Question**[49]. Leon, a Belgian Trotskyist, wrote his masterpiece at the age of 24, only two years before he died in an Auschwitz gas chamber at the hands of the Nazis in 1944.

Leon's central thesis is that the survival of the Jewish people could only be explained by the distinct socio-economic role which they played within particular societies. In the process of presenting his argument he establishes two distinct periods and types of anti-semitism. One he links to 'decaying feudalism', the other to 'rotting capitalism'. He associates the latter with the racism of the late nineteenth and early twentieth century. Leon's analysis is important because it establishes that anti-semitism, like racism, is variable in nature and degree. It can only be understood if it is placed in its correct and specific historical context.

In the ancient world the strategic location of Palestine assisted those of its inhabitants who became traders. Judaism was the religion and Hebrew the language of a vast trading community spread across the Mediterranian. The more that individual Jews outside Palestine moved into occupations distanced from trading the more they lost their distinctive Jewishness. Leon provides a number of examples and concludes:

> The law of assimilation might be formulated as follows:
>
> Wherever the Jews cease to constitute a class, they lose, more or less rapidly, their ethnical, religious and linguistic characteristics; they become assimilated.[50]

Under feudalism, during the early middle ages, the Jews continued to prosper. In a society dominated by agriculture they filled a special role, as merchants, providing luxury items, including slaves, for the nobility. Increasingly a second role, that of usurer or money lender, was added to that of the merchant. Only the merchant had the 'necessary cash for the rich noble wastrel'. He alone could help the King to fund an army, and when the peasant required cash urgently he too turned to the merchant-cum-usurer.[51]

During the eleventh century this situation began to change. A new class of non-Jewish merchants began to develop. They had one important advantage over the Jews: they engaged in production as well as trade. These embryonic capitalists produced for exchange the woollens of England, the cloths of Flanders, the salt of Venice. These merchants were able to displace the Jewish traders, but for a period the Jew was able to survive as money-lender. 'If during the preceding period "Jew" was synonymous with "merchant", it now begins increasingly to be identified with "usurer",' writes Abram Leon.[52]

Deprived of their role as merchants, the Jews were now vulnerable to attacks from their debtors, and in country after country they began to suffer from persecution. In 1189 Jews were massacred in London, Lincoln and Stafford, and a year later, besieged in York, large numbers committed suicide. Eventually, the state discovered that the benefits which Jews provided (loans and, by taxing them, a source of revenue) were outweighed by the disadvantages (debt, interest payments, and the resentment of the nobility and masses). Furthermore, the rulers of the more advanced countries could find alternative sources of revenue, and if they expelled the Jews they could expropriate their wealth. In 1290, the entire Jewish population of England, 3000 people, was expelled. In France, where the Jewish population was larger and the economy less developed the final expulsion did not occur until 1394, and in Spain, not until 1492.[53] Driven out of western Europe, most Jews fled to the more backward countries of eastern Europe, particularly Poland and Turkey.[54]

Centuries later in western Europe, as the bourgeoisie achieved their victories over the old regimes, more liberal attitudes developed. Jews were no longer a threat, restrictions were reduced and assimilation encouraged. According to Leon, by the end of the eighteenth century half the Jews of Berlin had converted to Christianity in a period of 30 years.[55] Among the German Jews who converted was the father of Karl Marx, along with much of the Jewish intelligentsia. In Britain Benjamin Disraeli, who was baptised a Christian, was just one individual from a Jewish family who prospered in this period. Capitalism had begun the process of resolving the Jewish 'problem', but unfortunately for the Jews, capitalism was incapable of completing the task.

In eastern Europe, as in the west, the breakdown of feudalism and the extension of the market economy was accompanied by an attack on the old Jewish merchant class. In the east, however, the process was much sharper, because the non-Jewish bourgeoisie was able to take advantage of the new techniques of industrial production developed in the west. The Jewish artisans also suffered. They could not compete with machine-made goods, and lost out in the battle for factory jobs at the hands of the peasant masses newly arrived in the cities.[56] Economically forced out of their old positions, the Jews were frequently prevented from entering the new economy by methods which eventually included the dreaded *pogrom*.

In Russia and then in Poland thousands of Jews were forced out of employment, brutally attacked and their homes and property looted and destroyed. After 1881 the *pogroms* grew worse and many of the Jews were forced to flee. In the next fifty years nearly four million Jews enmigrated; this from a world Jewish population which was less than eight million in 1880 and only about 14,800,000 in 1925. They settled in the more industrialised towns in the west where most of them joined the ranks of the industrial working class. The United States received by far the largest number of Jewish *emigrés* — nearly three million. 210,000 went to Britain, and 100,000 or more to each of Argentina, Canada, Germany and France.[57]

In the west capitalism was ailing, incapable of easily absorbing the new immigrants and only too willing to find scapegoats for its problems. Anti-semitism, typified by the Dreyfus affair in France, was the norm at the end of the nineteenth century, not the liberal attitudes and assimilation of the earlier years. As Leon wrote:

> The Jewish masses found themselves wedged between the anvil of decaying feudalism and the hammer of rotting capitalism.[58]

The earlier anti-semitism, associated with the breakdown of feudalism, tended to be justified in terms of the then dominant ideology, Christianity. By the nineteenth century the racial ideologies developed by men like Gobineau and Pearson, and encouraged by the imperialists, had become popular, and it is hardly surprising that they were adopted and adapted by the growing band of anti-semites.

Ruth Benedict argues that: 'During the Middle Ages persecutions of the Jews, like all medieval persecutions, were religious rather than racial. Intermarriage between Jews and Gentiles was condemned, not as a racist measure, but in the same manner as marriages between Catholics and heretics were condemned.' She adds: 'As racist persecutions replaced religious persecutions in Europe, however, the inferiority of the Jew became that of *race*.'[59]

This was more than just a shift in the dominant ideology from religion to race — the use of differences of race, rather than religion to justify anti-semitic persecutions. The nature of the persecution was different. Even the concept of *Jew* was different.[60]

As we have seen, religious anti-semitism was, at least in the more developed parts of Europe, primarily an attack on usurers. Jew and usurer were synonymous. In those instances where Jews had become 'real landowners', they also, according to Leon, sooner or later changed their religion.[61] Where they were no longer usurers they were no longer the object of persecution.

The racial anti-semitism which began to take root in western Europe in the 1890s had a very different character. It was not an attack on a socio-economic group, but on certain workers, certain shop-keepers and certain capitalists. Furthermore, those being attacked were not defined on the basis of practising a certain religion, but on the basis of being descended from people who practised a certain religion — an inherited, not an acquired characteristic. This is the meaning of *racial* anti-semitism. Jews were attacked not for what they did, but for who their forefathers were.[62]

In Britain, anti-semitism lurked behind the anti-alien movement which developed in opposition to poor, mostly Jewish, immigrants.[63] The Association for Preventing the Immigration of Destitute Aliens (APIDA) was established in 1891. Its executive included the Earl of Dunraven as president, a duke, two earls and two ladies as vice-presidents, and a host of MPs.[64] However its failure to involve any section of the masses from the East End of London, where most of the poor Jews and other recent immigrants had settled, helped to ensure its early demise a year later. According to one historian, 'the costermongers [stall-holders] together with the tradesmen, constituted the most bitterly and actively anti-alien group in London. Avowed anti-semitism, studiously avoided elsewhere, was only among these two groups a common and accepted thing.'[65]

The response of the working class was, at this stage, ambivalent. On one occasion, Ben Tillet, the dockers' leader, came perilously close to open anti-semitism, when he argued that the English were being pushed out of certain trades, 'as the Jews, or at least the foreigners, get to monopolise them.'[66] However in general there was sympathy for poor Jewish workers, combined with antipathy towards 'alien' immigrants. The fact that the poor Jewish workers and the 'aliens' were, in practice, the same people meant that there was an unresolved contradiction.

This ambivalence helped to undermine the opposition to a new offensive against the 'aliens' launched in 1901. In that year Major Evans-Gordon, the newly-returned MP for Stepney in East London, launched the British Brothers League.[67] Up to 6000 people attended League rallies and they were stewarded by 'big brawney stalwarts, dock labourers, chemical workers from Bromley and operatives.'[68] In 1902 they ran a petition campaign calling for immigration control, and collected 45,000 signatures from the residents of Tower Hamlets, which was one-tenth of the area's population. It was this agitation which culminated in the passing of the Aliens Act of 1905, the first modern anti-immigrant legislation, which was aimed, principally, at restricting the entry into Britain of Jewish workers.

Why was the British Brothers League so much more successful

than APIDA? By 1901, unemployment was, once again, rising. However, the main underlying cause of discontent seems to have been provided by housing shortage and high rents. The 'aliens' were conveniently, although falsely, blamed for both, thereby deflecting responsibility from the government and landlords.

At the same time there had been a long lull in the class struggle. The East End of London was, between 1888 and 1892, one of the main scenes of the New Unionism, the rapid spread of union organisation to unskilled and low-paid labourers. The great dock strike of 1889 ensured that the East End would provide a focus for this and for the socialist organisation which it inspired. This was not an atmosphere in which the anti-alien agitation of APIDA could flourish.[69] There followed, however, a long series of defeats for workers, culminating in the 1901 Taff Vale judgement which effectively withdrew legal immunities from the trade unions. The resulting climate of demoralisation, and the chauvinist mood encouraged by the Boer War of 1899-1902, provided the conditions in which the anti-alien campaign could win working-class support.

Racial anti-semitism thus had much in common with the anti-immigrant racism which developed in Britain first against the Irish, and more recently against Blacks. Jewish immigrants were seen by many workers as competitors, particularly for jobs and housing. They were blamed for deteriorating working and living conditions.[70]

However there are aspects of this racial anti-semitism which mark it out from other forms of anti-immigrant racism. First, in both Germany and Britain, before racial anti-semitism acquired a base among workers it already had support from a section of the middle classes. The non-Jewish traders and businessmen engaged in a fierce competition with their Jewish counterparts. Unlike the workers they did not have the experience of united class struggle to help undermine the tendency towards anti-semitism. As a class they could provide a real material base for anti-semitism, and this became more important as economic conditions worsened.

Second, new ideologies always make use of old material, and the new, racial anti-semitism was no exception. The Jews were, once again, held responsible for the death of Christ. More significantly, the racists increasingly adopted the 'capitalist parasite' as their stereotype Jew. Even Tillet attacked 'the *Jew*, as the most consistent and determined money-getter we know'.[71] Similarly John Burns, another leading trade unionist, while defending poor Jews, attacked the rich, 'stock-exchange Jews'.[72] This apparently radical rhetoric helped to perpetuate a mistaken notion of the typical Jew (most Jews were now in fact workers, at least in Britain), and in time this could be used to deflect attention from the real problems created by capitalism in general.

Fascism

Anti-semitism is not an essential component of fascist movements. The Italian fascist dictator Mussolini, for instance, embraced anti-semitism only in 1938, many years after he had come to power.[73] Daniel Guérin says that this was 'in imitation of ... Hitler, and to distract attention from ... current difficulties.'[74] Mussolini built the Italian fascist movement on the basis of national chauvinism and anti-communism. In the early days Jews were encouraged to join the fascist party. Perhaps the small number of Jews in Italy — between fifty and sixty thousand — made it difficult to use them as scapegoats.[75]

In Britain some of the fascists of the 1930s, such as Arnold Leese of the Imperial Fascist League, were undoubtedly anti-semitic.[76] However it is said of Oswald Mosley, leader of the British Union of Fascists, that his anti-semitism was '100 per cent insincere'; that he made use of anti-semitism to maintain the allegiance of his followers.[77] But anti-semitism did play a crucial role in the most important fascist movement, in Germany.

Fascism is essentially a mass movement of the middle classes, built in a period of defeats for the working class and under the impact of extreme social crisis. It provides a political regime based on the systematic repression and atomisation of the working class, in conditions where even the most basic trade union organisation is incompatible with the profitablilty of capital.[78]

In Italy the massive growth of Mussolini's fascists occurred only after the defeat of 1920, when workers had seized control of the factories. In Germany the defeats of 1919-1923 had weakened the workers' movement, which was further handicapped by the Communist Party's policy towards the Social Democrats, who they called 'social fascists' and reviled along with the Nazis. Following the economic collapse of 1929, production slumped by 42 per cent, unemployment rose by one million in January 1930 alone, and business after business went to the wall. The workers' movement was on the defensive, and, in despair, the petty bourgeoisie turned to fascism. Support for Hitler's Nazi Party rocketed.

Anti-semitism helped the Nazis to build a base among the petty bourgeoisie. Leon argues that 'the primarily commercial and artisan character of Judaism, heritage of a long historical past, makes it Enemy Number One of the petty bourgeoisie on the domestic market. It is therefore the petty-bourgeois character of Judaism which makes it so odious to the petty bourgeoisie'.[79] He adds: 'The economic catastrophe of 1929 threw the petty-bourgeois masses into a hopeless situation ... The petty-bourgeois regarded his Jewish competitor with growing hostility.'[80]

At the same time, because of the false association between Judaism and 'finance capital', the petty bourgeoisie could express their antagonistic relationship with big business by attacking 'Jewish capitalism'. Leon argues that because the petty bourgeoisie has an intermediary class position, between big business and the working class, it 'wants to be anti-capitalist without ceasing to be capitalist.'[81] It does this by distinguishing between 'good' capitalism and 'bad' capitalism. The Nazis were able to take advantage of this by defending 'national productive capital' and attacking 'Jewish parasitic capital'. Leon concludes:

> It is in its aspect as a capitalist element that the petty-bourgeoisie fights
> its Jewish competitor, and in its anti-capitalist aspect that it struggles
> against 'Jewish capital.'[82]

The attack on 'Jewish capital' assisted the Nazis in relating to the anti-capitalist instincts of German workers, which were much stronger than those of the petty bourgeoisie. The 'radical' appeal of the Nazis, at least until 1933, should not be underestimated. It was even indicated by their full name: the National *Socialist* German *Workers* Party. Guerin says that 'National Socialism's trick is to transmute the anti-capitalism of its followers into anti-semitism.'

Anti-semitism had one further role. Once Judaism had been established as the main enemy, anti-semitism could be used to justify German expansionism. 'The Jew' was to be found in a variety of guises — the Russian bolshevik, the Anglo-saxon plutocrat, and so on — and he would need to be challenged wherever he existed.[83]

Finally, anti-semitism was an important component of a Nazi racial 'philosophy' which justified 'Aryan' supremacy, but also the need to develop 'Aryan' racial purity. As Guérin puts it: '... anti-semitism, which began as a racial prejudice exploited as a demagogic trick, ended in the most abominable genocide of all time.'[84] The Nazi holocaust, in which six million Jews perished alongside an equal number condemned either as political opponents of Hitler or as members of other 'inferior' groups such as Slavs, gays, gypsies and the mentally ill, represented racism — and capitalism — in their most extreme and barbarous form. Its memory should underline just how urgent it is that we understand and combat racism. Today, however, fascist movements are more likely to exploit anti-black racism rather than anti-semitism.[85]

Chapter 2:
Racism and Immigration

IN THE past thirty years opposition to immigration has provided the main focus of racism in Western Europe. In 1945 there were only 25,000 black people in Britain. However, racial prejudice was well established and widespread. Following the war, and flushed with victory, most of the British felt they belonged to a superior 'race'. It was generally assumed that the British were at the top and black people were at the bottom. Such views were common in ruling circles, but widely held also among workers. They were a legacy of Britain's imperialist past.

On occasion, this racial prejudice had helped to encourage violence against Britain's small black population. For example the race riots of 1919, when, in the social unrest which accompanied the end of the First World War, anti-establishment aggression was sometimes diverted and turned against black servicemen and sailors. In Liverpool, during three days of tension, mobs of up to 7000 Whites chased and attacked every black person in sight. One black seaman was thrown into a dock and stoned to death. In Cardiff, where anti-black rioting lasted a week, three men were killed and dozens injured. Many of the rioters were *lumpen proletarians,* on the fringes of the working class, but they were led by soldiers. The inquest into the death of a young Arab killed by a lynch mob failed to determine whether his skull had been smashed by a chair leg or by a police truncheon. Riots also occurred in Manchester, London, Newport, Barry and Hull.[1]

As late as 1955, half of Britain's white population had never met a black person. However, more than two-thirds held a low opinion of black people or disapproved of them. They saw them as uncivilised heathens who practised cannibalism and polygamy, wore few clothes and lived in mud huts. They were thought to speak strange languages, to be illiterate, ignorant and inherently inferior. Black men were believed to have stronger sexual urges than white men, to be less inhibited and give greater satisfaction. These Whites objected vehemently to mixed marriages, working with Blacks, having Blacks in the house and to allowing Blacks to enter the country.[2]

This widespread racial prejudice was reflected in the views of government ministers. Cabinet minutes and other documents indicate that racism existed at the highest level. Furthermore, as we shall see, they demonstrate that the attitudes of Labour governments (1945 to 1951) and Tory governments (after 1951) were remarkably similar.

However, shortly after the end of the Second World War, the world economy entered a new and prolonged period of expansion. British industry soon encountered the problem of labour shortage. The King's Speech on the opening of parliament in 1951, the first written by a Tory government since the war had ended, declared: 'My government views with concern the serious shortage of labour, particularly of skilled labour, which has handicapped production in a number of industries.[73]

Attempts had already been made to secure increased supplies of labour without encouraging black immigration. In 1946, James Chuter-Ede, Home Secretary in the 1945 Labour government, told a meeting of the Cabinet Foreign Labour Committee that he would be 'much happier if the intake could be limited to entrants from the western countries, whose traditions and social background were more nearly equal to our own and in whose case it would be possible to apply the sanction of deportation'.[4]

Between 1946 and 1951 there were 100,000 new arrivals from Ireland.[5] Attempts to attract workers from Europe were largely unsuccessful, with one exception. By 1949 some 157,300 Poles had settled in Britain, encouraged by the Polish Resettlement Act, which allowed for the foundation of Polish hospitals, schools and other social and welfare organisations.[6]

This positive attitude was in marked contrast to that displayed towards black immigrants. George Isaacs, the Minister of Labour, said on the problem of finding accommodation for the new immigrants: 'If *our people* will not have *them*, we are up against a real difficulty'. It was 'self-righteously pointed out' by government spokespersons that to provide special welfare or housing facilities would discriminate against the existing population.[7] In June 1950 the government arranged for 'a review to be made of the further means which might be adopted to check the immigration into this country of *coloured people* from the British Colonial Territories'. Clement Attlee, the Prime Minister, favoured a ban on 'coloured' immigration. The review concluded that control legislation was unwise, although it might become necessary at a later date.[8]

At first the numbers of new black immigrants arriving in Britain were relatively small: no more than 2000 in any one year between 1948, when the *Empire Windrush* brought the first arrivals, and 1953. After this date there was a qualitative change and black immigration could be measured in tens of thousands per year.[9] The change was in part because some employers made special efforts to recruit in the West Indies and in India. These included London Transport and the National Health Service, then under the direction of Enoch Powell as Minister of Health.

As early as 1950 Cyril Osborne, Conservative MP for Louth, was calling for immigration figures for 'coloured' immigration, and asked questions about disease and crime, in a campaign reminiscent of that against the Jews half-a century before. In 1958, he told the House of Commons: 'It is time someone spoke out for the white man in this country ... I refer to the urgent need for restriction upon immigration into this country, particularly of *coloured* immigrants.'[10] Later he argued:

> Those who so vehemently denounce the slogan 'Keep Britain White' should answer the question, do they want to turn it black? If unlimited immigration were allowed, we should ultimately become a chocolate-coloured, Afro-Asian mixed society. That I do not want.[11]

For most of the 1950s Osborne remained on the fringe of British politics. The Cabinet considered his views, but rejected them. Government policy was essentially pragmatic: if you needed workers and the only workers you could get were black, you got black workers. They argued that immigration control might harm relationships with the colonies and commonwealth; there would be widespread opposition since there was no 'general public anxiety'; it would be difficult to discriminate against *'coloured'* immigrants and not restrict, for instance, Irish immigration.[12]

Pragmatism was no counter to prejudice, which continued at the highest levels. Harold Macmillan recalled that: 'Churchill rather maliciously observed that perhaps the cry "Keep Britain White" might be a good slogan for the election.' Churchill's comment was made partly in jest, but only partly. His racism was well known, certainly to his colleagues.[13] Nor was Churchill alone in his beliefs, as is indicated in this minute from a meeting of the Cabinet held after Churchill had left office:

> ... if immigration from the colonies, and, for that matter, from India and Pakistan, were allowed to continue unchecked, there was a real danger that over the years there would be a significant change in the racial character of the English people.[14]

From the beginning, the argument about immigration was about 'coloured' immigration. Labour considered the possibility of checking the immigration of 'coloured people'; the Tories thought it would be difficult to discriminate against 'coloured' immigrants; Osborne wanted restriction of 'coloured' immigration. When, on 1 November 1961, the government published its bill to control immigration (it became the 1962 Commonwealth Immigrants Act), everyone knew its purpose was to restrict 'coloured' immigration. Everyone knew this was a victory for the racists.

Despite this, many apologists for the 1962 Act (and subsequent anti-immigration laws) have attempted to justify the legislation in ostensibly non-racist terms. They argue that it is not a matter of race; there are just too many immigrants in Britain, and 'they' are taking 'our' houses, jobs and so on. This argument was always false. Between 1901 and 1961 there was a net *outflow* of two million people from Britain.[15] The net inflow of 12,000 between 1951 and 1961 seems tiny by comparison. Since the argument about numbers continued after 1961 it is worth comparing it to the net outflow of 320,000 between 1961 and 1971 and the net outflow of 306,000 between 1971 and 1981.[16]

The supporters of immigration control carefully ignored the fact that the 'immigrants' had come to Britain only because they were *wanted* in the factories and public services. A Cabinet minute of 3 November 1955 noted that it was 'the condition of full employment here that was attracting those immigrants'. The flow of immigration was controlled by the number of jobs available.[17] When the demand for labour diminished, the level of immigration began to decline. It fell from over 40,000 a year (1955-1957) to less than 30,000 a year

(1958 and 1959). When the numbers increased again in 1960 (57,700), 1961 (136,400) and the first six months of 1962 (94,900), the most important reason for this increase was that once immigration control seemed likely there was a panic, and 'immigrants' rushed to beat the ban.[18]

What were the real reasons for the Government's change of policy in favour of immigration controls? There were two, both related to the state of the economy.

First, labour shortage had become less of a problem. This was not a reason *for* introducing immigration controls, but it did mean that the argument *against* became much weaker. Even so, the 1962 Act only imposed limited controls. A voucher system was introduced: Category 'A' vouchers for those who had a specific job to go to, Category 'B' for skilled workers and professionals, and Category 'C' for unskilled and semi-skilled workers. Category 'C' vouchers were restricted in number.

Second, there had been a shift in public opinion. Animosity towards Blacks reached a high point in the 1958 riots in Nottingham and Notting Hill in West London. The youths responsible were officially condemned, but as Ruth Glass has argued: 'The trouble-makers of Notting Hill acted out tendencies which were latent in all strata. They were shouting what others were whispering.'[19] Much of the press and a number of Tory politicians were only too happy to provide an amplifier. They responded by linking violent attacks *on* Blacks to the need for immigration controls *against* Blacks. In the wake of the riots the *Daily Express* published an opinion poll which showed 79.1 per cent of those interviewed supported immigration control.[20]

The paternalist racism of empire was turning into racial hatred. Osborne and his friends were gaining followers for their politicisation of prejudice. But why? And why then?

The 1950s was a decade of boom, but material advance was not universal. In particular, although employment was expanding the government restricted expenditure on housing and welfare provision. Problems were particularly acute in the old inner-city areas, which is where many of the immigrants settled, replacing white workers who had moved out to more pleasant locations. Unfortunately, and partly because of media sensationalism and agitation by the far right, deprived Whites who had been left behind in the inner cities turned against even more deprived Blacks, rather than against landlords such as the notorious Rachman and their Tory friends. Sivanandan provides a valuable summary of the situation: 'the forced concentration of immigrants in the deprived and decaying areas of the big cities high-lighted (and reinforced) existing social deprivation; racism defined them as its cause.'[21]

At first the Tory government withstood pressure from the racists. The Tories entered the 1959 general election with a good deal of confidence. The economy was booming. 'You've never had it so good,' said Harold Macmillan. They were returned with an increased majority. Immigration was not an issue in the election.

Soon afterwards, however, the economy began to slow down. Unemployment started to rise. The centre of racist opposition to immigrants was Birmingham, where there were now layoffs in the car industry. As the economy faltered, incomes policy became tougher, the government's popularity declined, and with it their confidence. Eventually, in an attempt to regain the political initiative, they gave way to the racists.

The 1962 Commonwealth Immigrants Act was a major turning point, because it institutionalised racism. But it was not the end of the story. Immigration control was expected to reduce racism. The reverse happened. And with increased racism came further controls.

LABOUR'S SURRENDER

During the 1950s, the Labour Party's attitude to race and immigration was, in general, 'one of muddling through'[22] There were trade unionists, councillors and even MPs who sympathised with complaints about 'coloured immigrants', who articulated racist arguments, and who called for immigration control.[23] The leadership did not support them, but neither did they turf them out. They made no attempt to root out prejudice in the party.

Nevertheless, when the Tories moved to control immigration in 1961, Hugh Gaitskell, Labour's leader, rallied his party with a passionate defence of Commonwealth immigrants:

> What ... is the reason for the Bill? The immigrants are healthy, law-abiding and are at work. They are helping us. Why then do the government wish to keep them out? We all know the answer. It is because they are coloured ... There are social problems and an appalling housing problem. We concede the existence of these problems in certain areas,

but we do not believe for one moment that this Bill is the way to handle them ... But at the same time we think that it will do irreparable harm to the Commonwealth.[24]

Gaitskell was in favour of Commonwealth citizens having an *unconditional* right 'to enter this country at will.'[25] 'Unconditional' meant what it said: no health restrictions and no bar on criminals. Labour claimed, correctly, that the Bill was inspired by racist sentiment, and they opposed it *'in principle'*. Just before the final reading of the Bill, Denis Healey, Labour's front-bench spokesman, told a mass meeting of 'immigrants' in Birmingham, that he gave a *'solemn pledge'* that the Bill would be repealed by Labour.[26]

But even before the Bill became law, Healey was arguing that Labour would favour restrictions 'if the information collected by a serious survey of the whole problem revealed that immigration control was necessary.'[27] No longer was Labour holding to its position of opposition 'in principle'. The steady slide towards further controls and acceptance of the racist argument had begun.

The 1964 general election was won by Labour. They rapidly reversed their position on immigration controls. As had so often been the case, they said one thing in opposition and did quite another once in government. In November that year Sir Frank Soskice, the Home Secretary, presented Labour's new position:

... there should be no doubt about the Government's view. The Government are firmly convinced that an effective control is indispensable. That we accept and have always accepted.[28]

But why did Labour change its position? And why so quickly? The answer can be summed up in one word: Smethwick.

Smethwick was the West Midlands constituency where, in 1964, the Tory candidate, Peter Griffiths, ran a vicious racist campaign; one of the foulest, most venomous ever. He even condoned the behaviour of the gangs of children who went around shouting: 'If you want a nigger for a neighbour, vote Labour!'[29] The Labour candidate was Patrick Gordon Walker, a well established front bench spokesman. Just before the election he had issued a leaflet headed *'Urgent Stop Press'*, which declared:

Be Fair:

Immigrants only arrived in Smethwick in large numbers during the past ten years — while the Tory Government was in power. You can't blame Labour or Gordon Walker for that.

Labour favours continued control of immigration, stricter health checks and deportation of those convicted of criminal offences.[30]

Despite the fact that Gordon Walker was defending his own seat, despite his retreat on immigration, despite all this and more,[31] he lost the election. Nationally there was a swing to Labour of 3.5 per cent. In Smethwick there was a swing from Labour to the Conservatives of 7.2 per cent. Griffiths' demagogic racism had won him votes. The political lessons were not lost on the Tories,[32] nor on Labour.

Richard Crossman, later to be a Labour minister, had written in 1962: 'I am proud the Labour Party is leading the fight against the government's immigration Bill. We oppose it as a shameful piece of colour bar legislation.'[33] Now, in the wake of the general election, he confided to his diary:

> Ever since the Smethwick election it has been quite clear that immigration can be the greatest potential vote-loser for the Labour Party if we are seen to be permitting a flood of immigrants to come in and blight the central areas of our cities.[34]

Crossman was prepared to support a 'shameful piece of colour bar legislation' for one simple reason: votes. For Crossman, so for the Labour Party. There were few dissenters, and they failed to campaign against the Labour leadership. Instead of challenging reactionary racist ideas, the Labour Party had bowed down before them. Electoralism, not principles, is at the heart of Labour's politics.

Roy Hattersley was the only Labour MP to make a serious attempt to justify his conversion. He had already argued that Labour should have supported the Commonwealth Immigrants Act in 1961. Then in a speech in March 1965, he argued: 'I now believe that there are social as well as economic arguments and I believe that unrestricted immigration can only produce additional problems, additional suffering and additional hardship unless some kind of limitation is imposed and continued'. Hattersley subsequently proposed: 'We must impose a test which tries to analyse which immigrants ... are most likely to be assimilated in our national life.' He added that such a test would fall most heavily on people from Pakistan.[35]

The 'test' which was imposed by Labour was one which they had previously condemned — colour. Furthermore, in August 1965 Labour prime minister Harold Wilson attempted to upstage the

Tories by proposing new restrictions. The government had already stopped the issue of Category C vouchers. Now, Wilson proposed that Category A and B vouchers should be reduced to only 8,500 a year. Robert Moore has summarised the implications of Wilson's White Paper:

1. The White Paper conceded that black immigration *as such* was the problem.

2. It suggested that *numbers* were the essence of the solution to the problem and even went so far as to make the absurd suggestion that restricting black immigration would be good for race relations ... Once the debate is about numbers there are no issues of principle to be discussed, only *how many*.[36]

There was worse to come. Early in 1968 Asians living in Kenya were warned that unless they took out Kenyan nationality they could remain in the country only on a temporary basis. Many held British passports as Commonwealth citizens. On 8 February, Duncan Sandys, the right-wing Tory MP, predicted a sudden arrival of British Asians from Kenya. The following day, Enoch Powell put the figure at 200,000.[37] Such numbers never materialised, but the effect of such predictions was to stimulate a panic among British passport-holders in Kenya. This in turn panicked the Labour government, which introduced the 1968 Commonwealth Immigrants Bill, getting it passed through parliament in a day and a night.

The new law removed the right of entry and settlement in Britain from UK passport holders who lacked a 'close connection' with Britain.[38] Labour defined 'close connection' as birth in the United Kingdom or descent from a parent or grandparent born in the United Kingdom.[39] According to the Runnymede Trust: 'The "close connection" device was explicitly designed to ensure that white settlers in East Africa retained their right of entry to Britain by virtue of possession of a UK passport while black settlers, despite holding the same passport, did not.'[40] It was clearly racist, a fact acknowledged in Labour's 1978 Campaign Handbook.[41]

Crossman wrote that: 'A few years ago everyone would have regarded the denial of entry to British nationals with British passports as the most appalling violation of our deepest principles.'[42] There has been very little honest accounting about why they did accede to the racists' demands and 'violate' their 'deepest principles'. Crossman had little difficulty in justifying his position:

Mainly because I am an MP for a constituency in the Midlands, where racialism is a powerful force, I was on the side of Jim Callaghan [who argued in favour of the Bill].[43]

Labour's surrender had a disastrous effect. Until that point, the debate had been conducted within the normal framework of political controversy. The passing of the 1968 Act gave Enoch Powell the confidence to raise the stakes. The result was his notorious 'Rivers of Blood' speech in Birmingham on 20 April 1968. Powell quoted from racially prejudiced correspondence, unsupported by fact, to raise fears of an immigrant 'invasion'. He concluded:

We must be mad, literally mad, as a nation, to be permitting the annual inflow of some 50,000 dependents who are for the most part the material of the future growth of the immigrant-descended population. It is like watching a nation busily engaged in heaping up its own funeral pyre.[44]

The speech caused a sensation. Powell was immediately sacked from the Tory shadow cabinet. But, 'those who sought scapegoats had found a champion.'[45] In one opinion poll 82 per cent said that they thought Powell was right to make the speech, and 74 per cent agreed with him in general. He received 110,000 letters, mostly in support. Worst of all, 1500 London dockers marched to Parliament in his support. The following day, meat porters from Smithfield joined the protest.[46]

More concessions became inevitable. In 1969 Labour introduced a further Act which made it obligatory for dependents of Commonwealth immigrants to obtain an entry certificate before coming to Britain.[47] This ensured lengthy delays and increased hardship while people queued to join their families. Labour was making concessions to the racists all the way along the line. Paul Foot's conclusion is important:

One of the most constant rules in the history of immigration control is that those demanding controls are encouraged, not silenced, by concessions. The Commonwealth Immigrants act, 1968, far from stemming the tide, encouraged it still further.[48]

Edward Heath, the Tory leader, distanced himself from Powell's speeches, then moved rapidly to identify with their conclusions. The Tories won the 1970 general election and Heath, as prime minister, introduced the 1971 Immigration Act. The voucher system was scrapped, and with it any pretence that Commonwealth immigrants had any special rights. Primary immigration (that is, immigration of new workers, as opposed to dependents) was effectively halted. The Act provided a 'right of abode' in Britain for those it defined as 'patrial'. The Tory concept of 'patriality' was very similar to Labour's 1968 concept of 'close connection'. Both established rights on the basis of having a grandparent or parent born in Britain. In 1978 Labour commented:

> The 'patrial' yardstick gave the right of entry without restrictions to millions of Australians, Canadians and New Zealanders, who had previously not held UK and Colonies citizenship. It took it away from many members of the New Commonwealth since they were unlikely to have parents or grandparents born here, even though they had been full citizens of the UK and Colonies. Clearly numbers were not the decisive issue. It was colour.[49]

James Callaghan was right when he said that the 1971 Act gave 'a badge of respectability to prejudice'. He promised its repeal. In 1974 Labour was returned to government. Four years later, they had still not repealed the Act, though by then Callaghan was prime minister. That year, 1978, the Home Secretary, Merlyn Rees, was asked on the television programme 'Weekend World': 'What you really mean is that immigration control is a device to keep out coloured people?' He replied: 'That is what it is.'[50]

Labour had five years to scrap this 'device to keep out coloured people' which 'gave a badge of respectibility to prejudice'. They failed to do so. Why?

Under the Labour government there was a renewed racist offensive. In part this was a response to the results of the economic crisis, which deepened throughout the late 1970s. Unemployment rose from 500,000 to one and a half million. Inflation ate away at the real value of wages, while pay increases were held back by the 'Social Contract' between the Labour government and the trade union leaders. The 'social wage' was also cut, as health, education and welfare services were starved of funds.

The result was a real fall in working-class living standards, the first since the 1930s and the Depression. With workers' militancy against the employers also held back by the Social Contract, some began to look for scapegoats elsewhere. In May 1976 the racists, aided by press hysteria, were able to focus on the arrival in Britain of Asians from Malawi, where they had been faced with a situation similar to that in Kenya eight years earlier.

That month there were council elections. In Leicester the Nazi National Front received 16.6 per cent of the total vote. In Blackburn their rivals on the far right, the National Party, won two seats on the council; their eight candidates averaged nearly 40 per cent of the vote.[51] In June there were three racist murders following a particularly unpleasant speech by Enoch Powell.[52]

This new racist offensive encouraged the development of an anti-racist movement, but the Labour government did nothing to counter Powell and the fascists. On the contrary, they made further concessions. Callaghan had already sacked the relatively liberal Alex Lyon from the post of minister with responsibility for immigration. Under the new minister, Shirley Summerskill, there was an increase in deportations. These rose from 292 in 1974, the year Labour took office, to 714 in 1978. In March 1977 the government amended the immigration rules to prevent men from being accepted for settlement through marriages of convenience with women living in Britain. This meant increased 'marriage-snooping' by government officials. It also became known that immigration officials (not medical staff) were giving Asian women coming into Britain sexual examinations to determine whether or not they were virgins. Only after a series of public protests did Labour order that these tests should be stopped.

Labour's final contribution was to produce a government 'Green Paper' on nationality law. This included several proposals which were later incorporated into the Tories' 1981 Nationality Act. Labour's contribution was thus to lend credibility to the Tory arguments.

In sum, Labour's record in government has been a record of appeasement. They have implemented legislation which they have known to be racist; then at the behest of the racists they have introduced even more restrictive measures. They have justified their actions by arguing that these were aimed at improving race relations; the facts demonstrate that every concession has boosted the racists.

Labour's record is shameful. It is the record of a party more concerned to win the votes of racists than to challenge racism.

ARE NON-RACIST IMMIGRATION CONTROLS POSSIBLE?

British governments — Tory and Labour — have introduced and enforced racist immigration legislation. Those who oppose these racist controls fall into two groups: there are those who favour immigration controls, but oppose racist restrictions, and there are those who oppose *all* immigration controls. The first of these is identified with the Labour Party. According to the party's 1982 Programme:

> The repeal of the 1971 Immigration Act and the 1981 British Nationality Act will be among the highest priorities for the next Labour government. Over the last twenty years, our immigration laws and practice have become increasingly racially discriminatory, and a new nationality law has been based upon them. Our task will be to replace them with nationality and immigration laws and procedures which honour the obligations of the past; respect the family life of all those living here; do not discriminate on the grounds of race and sex; and are in accordance with the highest standards of human rights and civil liberties.[53]

The Programme refers to 'twenty years' of racially discriminatory legislation, which takes us back to the 1962 Commonwealth Immigrants Act, implying that the Labour Party now accepts that the 1962 Act was racially discriminatory. So does Labour plan to return to the situation before 1962, when Commonwealth citizens had an unconditional right of entry into Britain?

The answer is categorically '*no*'. Furthermore, although some of Labour's proposals are a little hazy, it seems unlikely they would even return to a pre-1971 or pre-1968 position. They appear to have no plan to scrap the racist notion of 'patriality' or the 'close connection' criteria of 1968. In addition the two and a half million British Dependent Territories citizens in Hong Kong (former citizens of the UK and Colonies) will certainly be deprived of any right of abode in Britain. They have yellow skins. On the other hand Labour will not remove the newly-acquired rights to full citizenship of the Gibraltarians and Falklanders, whose homes are also in the 'Dependent Territories'. They are white.[54]

In July 1986, David Waddington, the Tory Home Office minister with responsibility for immigration, launched a relatively mild attack on Labour's policies. He claimed that there could be a huge influx of Asians into Britain if Labour won the next election. Gerald Kaufman, Labour's shadow home secretary, responded for Labour by saying that the proposed changes would lead to an increase in immigration of no more than 1000 a year.[55] 'A Labour government,' he said, 'will maintain firm immigration controls, there's no doubt about that.'[56] Labour leader Neil Kinnock has made similar comments.[57]

How does Labour justify these 'firm immigration controls'? According to their programme they are opposed to controls on visitors, students, refugees and dependents.[58] They do, however, want to restrict the entry of those seeking employment, 'primary immigrants'. In the section on 'principles' in their Immigration Policy Statement they say: 'Immigration policy will continue to control, as part of economic planning, the entry of those who wish to come to work in Britain, but do not have overriding claims of family life or the need for asylum.'[59] The programme adds: 'In the near future it will not be possible for the economy to provide jobs for significant numbers of workers from overseas.'

This is the Labour Party's case for immigration controls. Purporting to be non-racist, it offers dangerous concessions to the racists. By setting out to exclude those who are looking for work, it accepts the notion of 'British jobs for British workers' — a slogan which the racists can follow to its logical conclusion by calling for the forced repatriation of all 'immigrants'.

Secondly, the idea that there is a 'need' to control immigration, panders to the racist vision of vast numbers of people flooding into Britain if controls were removed. This is false. As Hugh Gaikskell argued in opposing the 1962 Act:

> The rate of immigration is closely related, and in my view will always be closely related to the rate of economic absorption. There has been over the years an almost precise correlation between the movement in the number of unfilled vacancies, that is to say employers wanting labour, and the immigration figures ... It is in my opinion an utter an complete myth that there is the slightest danger or prospect of millions and millions of brown and black people coming into this country. Anyone who is trying to put that across is only trying to frighten people into believing it.[60]

Of course, socialists should defend the right of workers to seek employment where they wish, but in practice, very few unemployed people will leave Bombay to become unemployed in Bradford; just as the unemployed of Bradford rarely jump on a Jumbo to become unemployed in Bombay or Benidorm. The idea that they would is a concession to the scaremongering of the racists.

Any immigration policy — Labour or Tory — helps divert attention from the real source of social problems in Britain, by suggesting that immigration, and therefore 'the immigrants' are a problem. Bad housing, unemployment, and lack of spending on health, education and welfare have nothing to do with immigrants and everything to do with government policy and the current crisis of capitalism. This is what Labour argued in 1961. It is what they have, conveniently, forgotten today.

Labour's argument is hypocritical. Roy Hattersley, the party's deputy leader, is in favour of immigration controls, but opposes exchange controls. He favours restrictions on the movement of workers, but not on the movement of capital. He knows that the latter would provoke a reaction from bankers and big business which might undermine a Labour government.

Capital is therefore allowed to move from one part of the world system to another, in order to exploit the variations in the labour market. The rich may concentrate their wealth in the centres of big business — New York, Tokio, London, wherever they can reap the greatest profits, but when workers attempt to follow that wealth in order to escape poverty and unemployment, then up go the immigration barriers, with Labour's consent.

Socialists are internationalists, committed to putting the interests of workers before those of capital, whether private capital or in its guise as the 'national economy'. Workers, wherever in the world, whether black or white, male or female, young or old, should have the right to work, to a good standard of living, to housing, education and health — and the freedom to go wherever necessary in the world to obtain these rights. A worker from Calcutta should have as much right to a job in Coventry as a worker from Cardiff, or indeed Coventry itself. As socialists we believe in equality, and oppose all divisions between workers, particularly those based on nationality or race.

Many on the British left continue nonetheless to defend the idea of 'non-racist' immigration controls. For example, Vishnu Sharma of the Communist Party dismisses opposition to all immigration controls as 'a fatally defeatist position', and calls instead for a return to the position before the 1962 Act.[61] But neither he nor others taking this position explain what 'non-racist' immigration controls would be like.

Certainly Sharma's proposals would not amount to them. Before 1962 immigration was controlled by the Aliens Act of 1919, which discriminates against non-Commonwealth citizens. Can Sharma deny that the Commonwealth is a product of British imperialism? The 1919 Act, and its predecessor, the Aliens Act of 1905, were the product of anti-semitic agitation. Keir Hardie rightly denounced the 1905 Act as 'fraudulent, deceitful and dishonourable'.

Those who believe that immigration controls can be made non-racist have succumbed to the utopian dream of a capitalism without racism, without nationalism, without war. By doing so they have conceded the racist argument that 'immigrants' represent a problem for workers, diverting attention from the real enemy, capitalism.

Consistent anti-racism requires opposition to all immigration controls. Often taking this stand will mean isolation from the many white workers who accept racist ideas. Fear of this isolation leads sincere anti-racists to accept some form of immigration controls. But unpopularity is a lesser evil than making the slightest concession to the racist arguments which make Blacks the scapegoat for workers' problems. And — as we shall see — white workers can be won to anti-racist ideas, and must be won if the oppression suffered by black people is to be eradicated. To win them over, however, socialists must take a principled stance in opposition to all immigration controls as part of the struggle against the racist myths that justify them.

Chapter 3:
Racism Today

SINCE THE Second World War major economic and political changes have caused a shift in the character of racism in Britain. First, the British Empire is now dead, or virtually dead. Second, there are now more than two million Blacks in Britain, and the majority were born here. Third, Britain has changed from a country with a labour shortage to one with four million unemployed. Other factors are less tangible: on the one hand there has been the longterm impact of institutionalised racism; on the other the impact of trade union, black and anti-racist struggles.

How, then, has British racism changed?

One change is that racist ideologies no longer tend openly to denounce black people as inferior, but rather focus on the idea that Blacks have a culture and a way of life that is *different*. Enoch Powell, for example, the most important modern racist demagogue, actually denies that he is a racist:

> If by a racist you mean a man who despises a human being because he belongs to another race, or a man who believes that one race is inherently superior to another in civilisation or capability, then the answer is emphatically no.[1]

The key proposition of what some have called the 'new racism' is that 'people' (meaning white people) have a 'genuine fear' that the character of *'their'* country will be changed by the presence of too many people with an 'alien culture' (meaning non-white culture). This 'genuine fear', it is argued, is the product of 'human nature', so cannot be countered, and must be accepted as fact. The following could be regarded as the classic statements of the 'new racists'. The first is from one of Powell's infamous 1968 speeches, the second from Margaret Thatcher a decade later:

My judgement then is this: the people of England will not endure [a large number of 'immigrants']. If so, it is idle to argue whether they ought or ought not to. I do not believe it is in human nature that a country, and a country such as ours, should passively watch the transformation of whole areas which lie at the heart of it into alien territory.[2]

If we went on as we are, then by the end of the century there would be four million people of the New Commonwealth or Pakistan here. Now that is an awful lot and I think it means that people are really rather afraid that this country might be swamped by people with a different culture. And, you know, the British character has done so much for democracy, for law, and done so much throughout the world, that if there is a fear that it might be swamped, people are going to react and be rather hostile to those coming in.[3]

It is important, however, not to exaggerate the extent of the shift in the dominant form of racist ideology. It is certainly possible to distinguish between the racism of Thatcher and Powell, the *racism of difference*, and that of the 1940s and 1950s which generally assumed that Blacks were *inferior* and sometimes emphasised the danger of 'blood-mixing', but the racism of difference is far from new. The opposition to Jewish immigration early this century, for example, wsa not based on the belief that Jews were inferior — the contrary assumption was often made — but that they were 'aliens', in other words 'different'. Nor was it just the Tories who argued in this vein. Consider, for instance, the justification given by Labour Home Secretary James Chuter-Ede for opposing black immigration and encouraging 'entrants from the western countries, whose traditions and social backgrounds were more nearly equal to our own.'[4]

What is *not* said by the 'new racists', but nevertheless taken for granted, is often as important as what they do say. So, for instance, when Thatcher speaks of a 'different culture', many of her audience will assume that she means 'inferior culture', particularly as she goes on to argue that 'the British' have 'done so much for the world'. In addition, given a widespread acceptance of racial stereotypes, 'British character' will be understood by many to be a racial characteristic. In other words, although the Thatcher/Powell racism can be defended in terms of 'difference', it actually plays on ideas of superiority which were developed during the heyday of British imperialism.

The hidden language of superiority helps to strengthen the

allegiance of workers to 'their' state, and therefore to the ruling class. This becomes especially important during wartime, during the Falklands War for example, when the language of superiority may become more overt. Victory in these encounters then helps to reinforce the sense of superiority. The racism of empire thus continues to intertwine with anti-immigrant racism and its language of difference.

Racial prejudice

Alongside this shift in the dominant form of racist ideology there has been a rise in the general level of tolerance of black people among Whites. I am not arguing that there has been a decline in racism. Tolerance and prejudice concern the *opinions* which Whites hold about Blacks. These opinions may lead to some form of racist action — discrimination, support for a racist movement, violence against Blacks — but this is not inevitable.

What is the evidence for this increasing tolerance?

First, from time to time surveys have asked whether people considered themselves to be prejudiced. In the 1955 survey already referred to,[5] two-thirds of Britain's population considered themselves prejudiced, and half of these — one-third of the total — were 'deeply' prejudiced. By contrast, the British Social Attitudes survey of 1986 recorded 35 per cent of people who said they were 'a little prejudiced', while only 4 per cent said they were 'very prejudiced'.[6]

On the question of mixed marriages we can compare a 1958 Gallup Poll with the 1986 survey.[7] In 1958 mixed marriages between black and white were opposed by 71 per cent of the population; in 1986 between 50 and 60 per cent said they 'would mind' if a close relation were to marry someone of West Indian or Asian origin. More interestingly, in 1986 there was a marked difference between those aged over 55 — of whom two-thirds said they 'would mind' — and those in the younger 18-34 age group — of whom two-thirds said they 'would *not* mind'.

In 1958 and 1968 Gallup asked the question 'Should coloured people be allocated council housing?' In 1958 only 34 per cent of those interviewed said yes to this; by 1968 this had risen to 44 per cent.[8] In 1967 and 1968, just before and after the passing of the 1968 Race Relations Act, a series of opinion polls showed an average of 45 per cent supporting legislation against racial discrimination.[9] The 1986 Social Attitudes survey showed that 69 per cent supported the existing race relation laws.[10]

The detail of these statistics is not important — that is open to interpretation — but they do reveal that the trend since the 1950s has been away from racial prejudice and towards greater racial tolerance.[11] The present level of prejudice is still unacceptable, but there has been a change. Three factors have contributed to this shift in attitudes.

First, familiarity with black people has helped to eradicate some of the misconceptions held by white people. According to the 1955 survey, half of Britain's white population had never met a black person;[12] in 1958, when Gallup asked 'Do you personally know or have you known any coloured people?' only 49 per cent said yes.[13] In these circumstances it is hardly surprising that a large number of white people accepted many of the myths about black people.

Contact with black people has not, however, led automatically to an increase in tolerance. Experiences which tend to confirm existing prejudice are likely to be accepted, while those that contradict it can be treated as exceptions. There are a large number of white people who dislike Blacks in general, but are nevertheless friendly with the Blacks they know. This contradiction is likely to be reinforced by the material pressures of economic crisis. On the one hand there is pressure to consider Blacks in general as competitiors for jobs or housing; on the other there is a recognition that the man next door or on the next bench at work is in an equally unenviable situation as oneself, and is therefore a potential ally.

Secondly, over the past twenty years there have been many industrial struggles which have involved white workers and black workers fighting for their rights side by side. This has helped to teach the Whites that the Blacks were indeed their allies, demonstrating in a powerful way that the Blacks were part of the union, part of the working class. At the same time the employer was almost certainly white. It was class, not colour, which divided.

There have been times, however, when white workers have used their collective strength *against* Blacks.[14] It would be wrong to minimise the significance of these disputes, but it would be equally wrong to exaggerate their impact. Compared to the number of disputes where Blacks and Whites have stood side-by-side, the number where they fought against each other was small. Virtually every dispute in sectors of industry such as manufacturing — particularly the car industry — the railways and the buses, the health service and the construction industry has involved a significant number of black workers. David Smith's 1977 report **Racial Disadvantage in Britain** found that in one-third of the workplaces surveyed there had been at least one industrial 'stoppage' in the previous fifteen years, but only 0.6 per cent of those employing 'minority groups' had experienced 'industrial action over non-white employees'.[15] As Paul Foot concluded:

> In the main, throughout the numerous engineering factories and mills into which the immigrants were absorbed, the degree of hostility and bitterness at work was remarkably small.[16]

The third reason for increasing tolerance is that where Whites find their racial prejudice is challenged, they may initially react with resentment but over a period of time they are likely to change their attitudes. The challenge may take a variety of forms. At the lowest level it could be a fellow worker reacting against a racist joke. It might be black workers taking action against some discriminatory practice or against being treated as cheap labour. It might be Blacks and Whites being drawn together into some anti-racist campaign, as happened with the Anti Nazi League in the late 1970s. All these activities have helped to create a climate where racial prejudice is less likely to be tolerated.

Familiarity, class struggle, anti-racist action — all these factors have helped undermine racial prejudice. It is likely that the increased numbers of Blacks in Britain have tended to make Whites more tolerant, not less.

There is, however, another explanation: that the increase in racial tolerance has been due to the passing of laws against discrimination. It has been argued that although the Race Relations Acts have been ineffectual in preventing discrimination,[17] they have changed the climate of public opinion.

This explanation confuses cause and effect. As we have seen, attitudes were changing in advance of the legislation. For instance in April 1967 the country's two biggest trade unions, the transport workers (TGWU) and the engineers (AEU) changed their policy in favour of outlawing discrimination in employment. It was not until June that year that the Home Secretary announced that he would introduce a Bill to that effect.[18]

On the positive side, the legislation contributed to a process *which was already under way.*[19] It is worth noting that none of the three Race Relations Acts met with official Tory opposition. The Labour Party in particular, but also the Tories, supported the legislation because it provided a justification for backing racist immigration controls. As Roy Hattersley argued at the time: 'Integration without control is impossible, but control without integration is indefensible.'[20] Blacks would be kept out of Britain, but those already here had to be tolerated.

Moreover, politicians from both parties looked across the Atlantic and saw the development of the Black Power movement. They feared that a similar movement would develop in Britain unless action was taken to limit the extent of racism. The 1968 Act was preceded by a report on 'Anti-Discriminatory Legislation' which was based in particular on American experience. Among its authors was that well-known anti-establishment thinker, the future Tory cabinet minister Geoffrey Howe QC![21]

Furthermore, it was thought that race relations legislation could be used to help integrate a layer of black activists.[22] In the mid-1960s there were relatively few black people in the professions, not many black trade union officials and local councillors, and among West Indians few businessmen and religious leaders. As Sivanandan put it:

> There have been protestations that the [Race Relations] Board has failed. Failed for the black masses, yes. But it succeeded in what the state meant it to do: to justify the ways of the state to local and sectional interests — and to create, in the process, a class of coloured collaborators who would in time justify the ways of the state to the Blacks.[23]

The general rise in the level of racial tolerance may also have had an impact on the character of racist political movements. Although Cyril Osborne came from the right-wing fringe of the Tory Party, his campaign after 1958 for control of immigration was backed not only by broad sections of his own party, but also by a number of Labour MPs, trade unionists and councillors.By contrast, Enoch Powell's 1968 campaign lacked the backing of any significant Labour Party figure. Furthermore, as a result of his campaign, Powell found himself pushed out of the Tory shadow cabinet and on to the back benches.

After 1976 the racist initiative moved to the overtly fascist organisations, particularly the National Front. Powell still made speeches, but whereas in 1968 he did so as part of a challenge for the Tory Party leadership, in 1976 he was much more isolated. After 1976 racist marches became much more closely associated with the physical intimidation of black people. The racist movement had become narrower but nastier.

Institutionalised racism

Racist attitudes may have suffered some erosion since the 1950s — though one shouldn't underestimate the degree of prejudice which survives. Other forms of racism have, however, grown worse in the past thrity years. Of these the most important is *institutionalised racism* — the systematic discrimination against black people in jobs, housing, the legal system, and other aspects of social life.

Institutionalised racism is not merely a consequence of racist attitudes. It reflects the fact that the structures of society are so organised as to deny black people equal treatment with white. As Anne Dummett observes, 'racist institutions, even if operated partly by individuals who are not themselves racist in their beliefs, still have the effect of making and perpetuating inequalities'.[24]

The problems of racism which we face today are, in large part, the product of institutionalised racism in the past — which has helped to make rigid the inequality between black and white. This has now become a structural feature of society.

The boom that followed the Second World War created a massive expansion of the labour market. By and large, the better jobs were filled by Whites. Older workers were promoted, and higher and further education was expanded. The less desirable, less well paid jobs were filled by the new immigrants. They were willing to accept these jobs because they came from countries where employment prospects were bleaker,[25] and they were frequently prevented from obtaining the better jobs by discrimination. Hence the 1976 PEP report records that fewer than 1 per cent of white male graduates were employed in manual jobs, but that 21 per cent of 'minority' male graduates were manual workers.[26]

Detailed figures[27] show that in 1974 Whites dominated in professional and white-collar positions, and continued to do so in 1982. The proportion of white men in these categories in 1982 was still almost twice the proportion of black men. Black men were, and remain, overwhelmingly manual workers. They were more than twice as likely as white men to be in semi-skilled or unskilled jobs.

The most interesting change, over the eight years between 1974 and 1982, was the increase in the proportion of Blacks, and especially Asians, in the 'Professional, Employer, Manager' job category. This was particularly marked in the under-25 age group: 7 per cent of young white men were listed as 'Professional, Employer or Manager', as were 5 per cent of young West Indian men — but the figure for young Asian men was 18 per cent.[28] The development of this Black — or more specifically Asian — middle class is reflected in other statistics. For instance, according to the 1982 survey, 19 per cent of Asian men aged 16-24 had an A-level or higher qualification, compared to 12 per cent of Whites and 6 per cent of West Indians.[29] The majority, however, are still wage-labourers.

The 1972 figures show that Blacks coming to Britain were not only forced into lower grades of employment, but they also received the worst housing, typically in inner-cities. In 1974 only 1 per cent of Blacks lived in detached houses, compared to 21 per cent of Whites, while 66 per cent of Blacks lived in terraced housing, compared to 30 per cent of Whites. Blacks were twice as likely as Whites to live in accommodation which lacked exclusive use of a bath, hot water or inside WC.[30]

By 1982 the general picture of inequality was very similar, though there were some modest improvements. By now 3 per cent of Blacks were living in detached houses, with 59 per cent in terraced housing — the figures for Whites held steady.[31]

Inequalities in jobs and housing have a 'knock on' effect, perpetuating and intensifying other forms of inequality. In particular unemployment is higher for Blacks than for Whites: on average roughly twice as high.[32] Worst off are young West Indian men: in 1984 four in every ten were without jobs.

Probably the most important reason for the higher level of unemployment among West Indians and Asians is their concentration in lower job levels, which are more vulnerable to unemployment.[33] The concentration of Blacks in certain inner city areas, where there is high unemployment in general, has a similar effect.[34] Considering the decaying state of much of Britain's inner cities, these two factors are undoubtedly linked.

The other major factor affecting inequality in unemployment is undoubtedly straightforward racial discrimination. A 1985 PSI survey, **Racial Discrimination: 17 years after the Act**,[35] showed that roughly one third of employers discriminated against Blacks. The figures were similar for Asians and West Indians — and it was slightly higher than that found by a similar study carried out in 1973-4. In 1985 Peter Bottomley, a junior employment minister in the Tory government, admitted that between fifty and a hundred thousand young black people were unemployed purely as a result of discrimination against them by employers.[36]

Structural inequalities combined with racism make their impact in other ways. For instance the higher crime rates among young Blacks, particularly West Indians, are clearly linked to their considerably higher levels of unemployment. This situation is then made worse by the racist attitudes of the police. The result is police harassment of young Blacks.

'Popular' racism

The problem for black people becomes circular. Being unemployed or having a rotten, poorly paid job makes it difficult to get decent housing. Living in a run-down area makes it less likely that children will obtain the more stimulating education that middle class school students can expect. Lack of qualifications makes it more difficult to get a decent job. Involvement in crime then becomes more likely; so too does mental illness. Both further reinforce the problems of finding employment.

This reality helps to maintain a popular image of 'the average Black' which fits closely with the old racist stereotype. Elements of the stereotype appear and re-appear through the racism of slavery, the racism of imperialism and anti-immigrant racism. Blacks are seen as villainous, ignorant and lazy. When they protest they are branded as ungrateful.

The historian Michael Banton has observed that 'Much of today's racial folklore is in fact the science of a century ago.'[38] This folklore is kept alive by statistics, presented by the 'authorities' — the police, government and media — often without comment as if they were objective facts and did not need explanation. Racist Whites are then left secure in their belief that unemployment levels among Blacks are high because Blacks are stupid, and so on. Explanations which show Blacks to be the victims of social conditions, on the other hand, are avoided.

Where necessary the facts are distorted. An example of this was the invention of the crime of 'mugging', in which statistics were manipulated in order to magnify the problem and then to provide a racial breakdown, even though this was not done for far more serious crimes. A further example was Margaret Thatcher's suggestion, after the 1981 riots, that in previous periods of high unemployment there had been no riots. This was just not true. There were major disturbances in the 1880s and the 1930s which involved unemployed Whites — and no Blacks. But Thatcher's argument was accepted by many people because of widespread belief in the racist stereotype that Blacks are more prone to violence than Whites. In the process, the stereotype was reinforced and attention diverted from the real causes of the riots: social inequalities and racist policing.

Racial stereotyping has other implications. Whites in positions of some authority, even if they are not consciously racist, can easily slide into dealing with black clients as if they were dealing with 'the average black', rather than with an individual. In return, the black person can respond by treating the civil servant, local government worker — not to mention the police officer — as 'inevitably racist'. Presumed differences then help to recreate the reality. In a hostile environment Blacks begin to fall back on their friends, family networks and 'ethnic' religions. This in turn becomes a further justification for the racist's view that 'they' are *different* from 'us'. The exceptions are ignored as are social and historical explanations. Instead assumptions are made about 'the nature of Blacks', that they have a different 'psychology', and although today it is not often expressed, the assumption that this is because of a different 'biology', a racial difference.

So Blacks suffer doubly from rotten material conditions — from the material conditions themselves and from the way those material conditions help to sustain racist assumptions.

The racist assumptions in turn help to reinforce the rotten conditions. Discrimination, police harassment, racial violence, all tend to force people back to the 'ghetto'. Thus structural inequalities help to sustain popular racism, which helps to sustain the inequalities.

Will the creation of a black middle class change the situation? This is extremely unlikely. Racists are quite capable of integrating a second stereotype — the Asian businessman — into their scheme.

Indeed the existence of a black middle class, particularly an Asian business class, can be used to stimulate racism amongst middle class Whites, who see them as competitors. This is what occurred in Germany in the 1930s. It is possible that Asians could replace the Jews as the modern scapegoat.

Blacks are concentrated in the lowest job levels and the worst housing, but it is important to remember that the majority of the unemployed, the majority of unskilled and semi-skilled workers, the majority of people in rotten housing are white. It is important to remember this because it is an indication of the fact that there is a unity of interests between working-class Blacks and working-class Whites.

Although, over the past thirty years, there has been an undermining of racial prejudice, particulartly among workers, institutional racism and structural inequalities remain and continually assist in the reproduction of popular racism. In addition, racism has been intensified by two further factors.

Firstly, the deepening crisis of capitalism encourages racism. The squeeze on resources — jobs, houses, profits — tends to sharpen the competition for whatever is available. Increased competition promotes increased racism. Furthermore, the crisis leads to increased social problems. More welfare claimants make more claims to fewer civil servants. There are more likely to be disputes between claimants and civil servants, and these are more likely to be interpreted in racial terms. Racism and high unemployment encourage periodic outbursts in the form of riots. When the police repress the disturbances their actions are justified in racist terms. And so on.

Secondly, the decline in industrial militancy since the 1970s means there have been fewer opportunities for workers to unite, and in the process to begin to overcome racism. With the decline in trade union organisation, workers are more likely to look for alternative solutions to their problems; solutions which do not involve collective action.

The picture looks depressing. How then can racism be fought?

RACISM IN THE 1980s

Before looking at strategies for fighting racism, let us first draw together the strands of our analysis.

It is possible to comprehend racism only if it is placed in the context of history. Once this is done, it becomes apparent that racism is not a static phenomenon: it has not always existed and its character is continually changing. The development of racism, and the different forms which it has taken, can be understood in relation to changes in the dominant forms of social relationships. Racism reinforces those relationships, but changes in social relationships will alter the nature and extent of racism.

More specifically, racism is a product of capitalism. Changes in the character of capitalist society have produced changes in the character of racism. Any significant challenge to racism must involve a significant challenge to the dominant social relations within capitalist society. The most significant challenge — the destruction of capitalism and the establishment of socialism — would provide the basis for the eradication of racism.

This analysis rules out certain views of racism.

First, Whites are not inherently racist. There is no evidence of racism in the ancient Mediterranean world. Moreover, as we shall see in the second half of this book, Whites have often fought alongside Blacks against racism.

Secondly, racism is not necessarily about colour at all. The Irish suffered, and to some extent continue to suffer, from racism in Britain. The Jews were so lacking in visible distinctiveness that the Nazis imposed the wearing of the star of David. It is even possible that a black person can be racist towards another Black. There have been cases of West Indian youths joining forces with gangs of racist white youths physically to attack Asian youths.

The dominant form of racism is, of course, White against Black, but this is because Whites tend to be in dominant positions, not because they are white. In 1983, when the Nigerian government expelled more than two million Ghanaians (between 50 and 100 died in the process) their behaviour bordered on racism. The oil boom had come to an end and the Nigerian government used the Ghanaians as a scapegoat for their problems. Radio Lagos commented: 'We cannot afford to watch these illegal aliens pollute our much-cherished traditional values'. The argument could have been borrowed from a **Sun** editorial, but it wasn't! It did not need to be. It is capitalism in crisis which promotes racism, and capitalism and the crisis are international.

Thirdly, racism does not arise because there are more than a certain proportion of people from a certain ethnic group in a particular area. In Britain there is little difference in the levels of racial prejudice from region to region, despite large differences in the proportion of Blacks in the local population. It is even possible that in areas where there is a high density of Blacks there is a lower level of prejudice among Whites. In the Bahia region of Brazil there is less prejudice against 'negroes' than in Sao Paulo, even though they are proportionately far more numerous there than in Sao Paulo. In Germany anti-semitism did not decline with the removal of the Jewish population.

Fourthly, racial oppression is not the same as religious oppression. Racism oppresses people on the basis of certain characteristics which are assumed to be inherited and assumed to be held in common. Religious oppression concerns acquired, not inherited, characteristics.

Fifthly, racism is not about a relationship between people from two equally matched groups. Thatcher may talk about *different* cultures, but she comes from a dominant group and assumes her culture (meaning 'race') to be superior. There is no such thing as 'reverse racism'. In other words, at least in Britain, black people cannot be racist towards Whites. Black people may be prejudiced or even violently anti-white, but these attitudes are a reaction against racism and should not be equated with racism.

Finally, the notion that racism is just about ideas is simplistic and mistaken. It certainly underestimates the importance of institutionalised racism. It is also wrong to separate the two elements of racism — popular and institutional — from the broader social structures which support them.

If this analysis is correct, then racism can only be eradicated as part of the struggle to replace capitalism with a socialist society. But black people have, when seeking their liberation, looked in other directions, either hoping to change society by organising separately from Whites, or using their electoral power to squeeze reforms out of the existing system. How well have these strategies worked in practice?

Chapter 4:
The Rise of Black Resistance

BLACK PEOPLE have often reacted to the racism of white society by organising separately from Whites. Sometimes this has become a strategy: black nationalism, according to which Blacks can free themselves only by organising separately. The rich experience of independent black organisation in the United States offers a test of this strategy.[1] What can we learn from black struggles in the US?

The American Civil War of 1861-5 represented, according to Marx, 'a conflict between two social systems: the system of slavery and the system of free labour'. The slave system of the southern states, producing cotton for the textile mills of Lancashire, had become an obstacle to the development of an integrated national economy dominated by the industrial capitalists of the US north-east. The South was defeated, and slavery abolished, in part because of the efforts of the slaves themselves.[2] In the period after the Civil War, when the South was under Federal military occupation, and the more radical Northern capitalists pursued a programme of reconstruction designed to achieve racial equality, poor Whites did, on occasion, make common cause with the freed slaves to common advantage.[3]

In 1877, however, Federal troops were withdrawn from the South, and the experiment of reconstruction ended. Northern capitalists allowed the plantation owners to re-establish their domination of the South. The Blacks, though formally free, were forced by their lack of land into sharecropping agreements which condemned them to the status of sweated labourers for white landowners. This new kind of forced labour was buttressed by a system of racial domination designed to terrorise the black peasants into submission and to keep them divided from the poor Whites. Laws were passed which enforced segregation and disenfranchised

Blacks — the 'Jim Crow' laws — and these were backed up by lynching parties and the Ku Klux Klan. It's hardly surprising that the first challenges by black people to their oppression should have developed among those who emigrated to the Northern cities, where they weren't subject to the acute reign of terror in Good Old Dixie. The first political expression of this struggle came after the First World War with the Garvey movement.

THE GARVEY MOVEMENT

Marcus Garvey was, and remains, a controversial personality. For some he was 'the black Moses'.[4] For others, he was 'a sheer opportunist and demogogic charlatan.'[5] Neither view was completely correct. Nor was either entirely wrong.

Garvey was born in Jamaica in 1887. In 1912, he visited London, where he became aware of a growing nationalist ferment, particularly in Ireland, Egypt and India. In his **Philosophy and Opinions** he wrote:

> I asked myself 'Where is the black man's Government?' 'Where is his King and his kingdom?' 'Where is his President, his country, and his ambassador, his army, his navy, his men of big affairs?' I could not find them, and I declared 'I will help to make them' ... I saw before me then ... a new world of black men, not peons, serfs, dogs and slaves, but a nation of sturdy men making their impress upon the human race. I could not remain in London any more.[6]

Garvey returned to Jamaica where, in 1914, he founded the Universal Negro Improvement Association (UNIA). His success was limited and in 1916 he moved to New York, to Harlem. Two years later he still had only 17 members.[7] But another two years, and Garvey was at his height. According to Harry Haywood, a critic of Garvey:

> While estimates of the organisation's membership vary — from half a million to a million — it was the largest organisation in the history of US Blacks. There can be no doubt that its influence extended to millions who identified wholly or partially with its programs.[8]

Garvey's newspaper, **Negro World**, became the most widely-read black weekly in America. Its worldwide circulation may have reached nearly 200,000.[9] The UNIA international convention in 1920 opened with a rally at Madison Square Gardens attended by 25,000 supporters.[10] Divisions and chapters of the UNIA existed in 42 countries, but it was primarily an American organisation, and that was where three-quarters of its divisions were located.[11] Its Harlem headquarters, Liberty Hall, had an auditorium with seats for 6000 people.[12]

To understand this phenomenal growth it is necessary to understand the summer of 1919. There had been a revolution in Russia. The First World War was over. There was a new mood, signalled by a general strike in Seattle and a strike by 365,000 steelworkers.[13] The working class was on the move, but their struggles were distorted by racism. The attempt by the Industrial Workers of the World (IWW) to build industrial unions uniting workers across race and trade had been crushed by the employers and the state, leaving the unions dominated by the racist and craftist American Federation of Labour (AFL). In most of these unions Blacks were prevented from organising alongside Whites. Worse,

> There were floggings, branding with acid, tarrings and featherings, hangings and burnings ... More than 70 Negroes were lynched during the first year of the post-war period. Ten Negro soldiers, several still in their uniforms, were lynched ... Fourteen Negroes were burned publicly, eleven of whom were burned alive.[14]

In 1919 there were 25 race riots. Historian Philip Foner says that in each of the seven major disturbances 'the initial violence came from Whites.'[15]

But the new mood had produced a 'new Negro'; 360,000 Blacks had entered military service, and in the five years after 1917 750,000 Southern Blacks had migrated north to find jobs in the great industrial centres. There was a new confidence and Blacks fought back. This can be seen from the official reports of the Chicago riot, which lasted thirteen days. Of the 38 persons killed, 15 were white; of 250 injured, 170 were white.[16]

Under the impact of the mass movement Garvey's speeches became more militant. 'We refuse to die without getting liberty', he thundered, 'and to get liberty we are prepared to die'.[17] At a speech in London he went further:

> Four hundred million black men are beginning to sharpen their swords for the war of the races ... and it will be the bloodiest war the world has ever seen. It will be a terrible day when the Blacks draw sword and fight for their liberty.[18]

Garvey had roused the masses, but where would he lead them? The 1920 convention passed a 'Declaration of Rights' which in essence was a charter of 'democratic' demands: justice in the courts, free elections, freedom of the press and of religious worship, an end to discrimination and so on. It also demanded Africa for the Africans at home and abroad.

Garvey's aim was to unify the 'race' by means of developing 'race pride'. To this end he established a chain of small businesses and encouraged black business in general. He attempted to stimulate national consciousness by introducing a national flag and national anthem, as well as by having a 'cabinet' elected with himself as President General. The colourful parades led by the Africa Legion militia and Black Cross Nurses gave force to his simple message, 'Up you mighty race'.

Garvey had a programme for creating a nation, but none for establishing a state. As early as 1921 he had begun to compromise and was arguing, 'the negro must be loyal to all flags under which he lives'. 'Back to Africa' was the only 'practical' solution he offered, and even he accepted that it would be possible only for a minority.

Garvey's success was in presenting a vision of a society where black people would be free from the domination of Whites. Sometime later, Leon Trotsky argued that this was a desire for self-determination which could only be fulfilled on the basis of revolutionary struggle.[19] There were those at the time who drew this conclusion. Foremost among them were Cyril Briggs and the African Blood Brotherhood. Briggs was a socialist who opposed the war and lost his job as editor of the **Amsterdam Times** for his pains. Briggs was inspired by the Bolsheviks and the Russian Revolution, but did not immediately join the American Communist Party when it was formed in 1920.

Briggs argued that for American Blacks to achieve equal rights, the liberation of Africa was necessary — and for this, Blacks in America would have to become stronger. His immediate concern was to link this nationalist struggle to the struggle for socialism.[20] His practice marked him off from Garvey in two distinct ways. Firstly, he defended, and may have organised, armed self-defence during the Tulsa riot of 1921.[21] Secondly, Briggs argued for black and white working-class unity. This provoked his split with Garvey and the UNIA. Briggs had become a revolutionary socialist and joined the Communist Party in 1921.[22]

Briggs did have an answer to problems facing American Blacks, but it was not particularly popular. At its height the Brotherhood had fewer than 5000 members.[23] In 1921 the idea of black and white unity to achieve black liberation and socialism must have seemed a fantasy: white workers were keeping Blacks out of their unions and participating in lynch mobs.

Garvey, by contrast, moved increasingly to utopian and reactionary solutions. His ideas *were* based on fantasy but must have seemed more attractive than those of Briggs. Even if he could provide no material benefits his vision could at least comfort the spirit. Consequently, for a few more years, he retained his mass popularity. C L R James has explained this paradox:

> What was Garvey's programme? Back to Africa. ... It was pitiable rubbish, but the Negroes wanted a lead and they took the first that was offered them. Furthermore desperate men often hear, not the actual words of an orator, but their own thoughts.[24]

Bit by bit Garvey came unstuck. Incapable of securing a base in Africa by force, he attempted to negotiate a settlement with President King of Liberia. But the Liberian government was bankrupt. In order to support the luxurious lifestyle of King, his family and supporters, they simply sold up to the highest bidder: the Firestone Rubber Company. In June 1924, when a team of UNIA experts arrived in Liberia to prepare for the arrival of the first 500 colonists they were not even allowed to land.

In 1919 Garvey's standing had been enhanced by his launch of the Black Star Shipping Line and the purchase of three ships. Only Blacks were allowed to buy shares in the company. The ships were bought for far more than they were worth. The line, either through incompetence or malice, was badly run, and the ships were either abandoned or sold. By 1922 the company had folded. Unbowed, in 1924, Garvey founded a new shipping line, the Black Cross Navigation and Trading Company. Its only ship, the *Booker T Washington*, was the hit of the 1924 UNIA convention, but did not survive its inaugural voyage. Garvey's venture eventually foundered on his inability to sell sufficient stocks.

By this stage, Garvey had been found guilty of fraud, on the single count that he continued to sell stock in the Black Star Line knowing it to be insolvent. He appealed, but lost and began a five-year prison sentence. Garvey's supporters claim that he was innocent. This is not the main point. Garvey's was effectively a political trial, and the verdict a political defeat. The Attorney General had been encouraged to begin the trial following receipt of a letter from a 'committee of eight' prominent Americans who represented the élite of black America. They included Robert Abbott, the wealthy publisher of the mass circulation Chicago **Defender**, William Pickens of the liberal establishment's National Assocation for Advancement of Coloured People (NAACP)[25], and Chandler Owen, a leading trade unionist and Socialist Party supporter.

Garvey aimed to 'unite the race' behind the UNIA. Others, representing a variety of backgrounds, but particularly the black middle classes, wanted to be assimilated into American society and were determined that 'Garvey must go'. The contradictions of the Garvey movement's politics enabled them to re-establish their base among the poorer sections of black America.

Garvey argued in favour of 'racial purity' and against sexual relationships between the races. He once attacked Briggs as a white man 'passing for negro'.[26] Interestingly he referred to his supporters as 'Zionists'. This was not intended to flatter his Jewish supporters, of whom there were a significant number, as he was known to be prejudiced against Jews.[27] Some years later, after Mussolini's troops had overrun Ethiopia, he claimed, 'We were the first fascists.'[28]

Garvey's concern for 'racial purity' was mirrored by that of the Ku Klux Klan, for which he clearly had some respect. 'I regard the Klan, the Anglo-Saxon Clubs and white American Societies', he stated, 'as better friends of the race than all other groups of hypocritical whites put together'. Since Garvey and the Klan shared a common vision — segregation — it is hardly surprising that in 1922 he should have met with their 'Imperial Giant'. This provoked much dissent within the UNIA, and Garvey's biographer suggests that the meeting was a tactical blunder. This may be so, but it flowed from the logic of his politics.[29]

Garvey's attitude towards the Klan should be contrasted with his antipathy towards white workers and trade union organisations. He saw white workers as competitors for jobs, and argued that the black worker 'should keep his scale of wage a little lower than the Whites', and thereby 'keep the goodwill of the white employer'. 'The white capitalist', said Garvey, was the black worker's 'only convenient friend'. This position did not endear him to those Blacks busily attempting to build union organisation.[30]

C L R James has rightly argued that 'the Garvey movement ... looked to Africa because there was no proletarian movement in the United States to give it a lead'.[31] Instead the lead was given by a down-trodden layer of the petty bourgeoisie. They dreamt of a bourgeois democracy free from racial oppression, but feared the conflict with the American state which was necessary to achieve such a change. Their utopian nationalism reflected their dilemma. As Christina Baker put it:

> ... nationalism can be progressive, or it can serve as a limiting force. In the case of Garveyism, it was double-edged. Many joined the UNIA or considered themselves Garveyites because the idea of Black pride and dignity was so important. This was a step forward. But with the decline of mass activity, Garvey failed to provide any real alternative for Blacks. Instead, Garveyism served as a block to Blacks realising the real motor of the system and the way forward for themselves and other workers.[32]

AMERICAN COMMUNISTS AND THE BLACK STRUGGLE

The racism prevalent in the official institutions of the American labour movement — the AFL and the Socialist Party — was one reason for the appeal of Garveyism among Blacks. But there had always been another tradition within the working class in the US, represented by the Knights of Labour and the 'Wobblies' (the IWW) among others, which fought for a united working-class struggle against capitalism. The Russian Revolution stimulated American revolutionary socialists committed to this strategy to organise independently in the Communist Party.

The Communist International, under the influence of Lenin, Trotsky and other Bolshevik leaders, insisted as a matter of principle that its sections should take the lead in combatting national and colonial oppression. The session of the Second Congress of the Comintern, held in Moscow in August 1920 and devoted to the national and colonial question, was introduced by Lenin.

Among those who spoke was John Reed, one of the founders of the American Communist Party. He described in detail the appalling oppression to which Blacks in the US were subjected, and the beginnings of their struggle to free themselves. He concluded:

> The Communists cannot stand aloof from the Negro movement, which demands their social and political equality and at the moment,

at a time of the rapid growth of racial consciousness, is spreading rapidly among the Negroes. The Communists must use this movement to expose the lie of bourgeois equality and emphasise the necessity of the social revolution which will not only liberate all workers from servitude but is the only way to free the enslaved Negro people.[33]

Unfortunately, the first attempt by the American Communist Party to develop a strategy for the struggle against racial oppression took place *after* the degeneration of the Russian Revolution, when Stalin was establishing his dominance over the international Communist movement. In 1928, following the Sixth Congress of the Comintern and under Stalin's influence, the party adopted the demand for 'Self-determination for the Black Belt'. The Black Belt was an area of the southern states, 1600 miles long and 300 miles deep, where the black population was heavily concentrated. It included parts of twelve states — in some counties Blacks were the majority, in others a substantial minority.[34] 'The Communists are for a Black Republic' the party declared, and began publishing maps showing its boundaries.[35]

Trotsky, in discussions with his American supporters and with C L R James, explained what was wrong with this approach. 'The Negroes', he argued, 'are a race not a nation. Nations grow out of racial material under definite conditions ... We of course do not obligate the Negroes to become a nation; whether they are is a question of their consciousness, that is, what they desire and strive for.'[36] Six years later he said this:

> I do not propose for the party to advocate, but only to proclaim our obligation to support the struggle for self-determination if the Negroes themselves want it ...
>
> So far as I am informed, it seems to me that the CP's attitude of making an imperative slogan of it was false. It was a case of the Whites saying to the Negroes, 'You must create a ghetto for yourselves.' It is tactless and false and can only serve to repulse the Negroes. Their only interpretation can be that the Whites want to be separated from them.[37]

The Communist Party's 'self-determination' slogan of 1928 was mistaken, but it probably had a positive spin-off. Mark Naison argues in his important study **Communists in Harlem** that although it was 'an albatross' round the party's neck, 'a singularly poor mobilising device in the North and the South,' it 'endowed the black struggle with unprecedented dignity and importance. At any rate, it was only after 1928 that the Communist Party paid serious attention to work among Blacks. In the north, where most of this work was concentrated, the main demand was for 'equality'.[38]

The party encountered two major problems with its activity among Blacks. First there was a credibility gap. Why should the Communist Party be different from any other predominantly white organisation? Why should they be trusted? Secondly, there were problems of the party's own making: reliance upon tactics determined in Russia. There were some notable achievements in tackling the first problem — but the good work was eventually undone by subservience to the Stalinist bureaucracy in Moscow.

How did the Communist Party, whose members were overwhelmingly white, relate to Blacks in areas such as the Harlem district of New York? Their work was helped by a decision, taken in 1925, to reorganise the party into street units (neighbourhood branches) and shop units (factory branches), grouped together under section committees. Previously the members of the foreign language federations, who comprised 95 per cent of the party's membership in 1922, had worked separately from the black members, but these organisational changes helped break down sectional divisions and provided a large number of members who could begin to work with Blacks in areas such as Harlem. Although the Harlem section was led by Blacks, most of its members were white, and they made a substantial contribution to building the organisation. As late as mid-1933 there were only 87 Blacks in a section of 560 members. Eighteen months later 300 of the 1000 members were black.[39]

The party leadership wanted the Harlem section to be 'thoroughly interracial, with Blacks and Whites sharing a common social and cultural life as well as participating in joint struggle'. Naison suggests that such a development 'represented something of a landmark in American race relations.'[40] Inevitably there were problems. On one occasion the party's central committee decided to dramatise its determination by holding a public trial of one of its members, whom they charged with white chauvinism. It was held in Harlem and 1000 people attended. At the same time, leading black members were expected to 'conduct tireless activity among the rank and file Negro comrades against all remnants of distrust, suspiciousness and supersensitiveness...to white revolutionary workers'.[41]

The case of the Scottsboro Boys provided the party with an

opportunity to demonstrate their commitment to fighting racism. The nine boys were arrested in March 1931 on the trumped-up charge that they had raped two white girls. The Communist Party despatched lawyers from International Labour Defence, and developed a close and important relationship with the boys and their parents. Meanwhile, the NAACP dithered, not wanting to be too closely associated with possible rapists. To begin with the demonstrations against the trial were mostly white, and mostly party members. In the summer of 1932 the party made a pragmatic shift in their line and initiated the Scottsboro Unity Defense Committee. This, together with minor legal victories and sheer persistence, enabled them to mobilise a new layer of Blacks in Harlem. Despite mistakes, the party's credibility increased enormously as a result of the Scottsboro Case.

Unemployment was a major issue which the party had to confront. Not only was unemployment higher among Blacks than among Whites, but many Harlem stores refused to employ black workers. In 1934 the Garveyites initiated a picket of Harlem's leading store, Blumsteins, and demanded the replacement of white workers with Blacks. The Communist Party responded by mobilising Whites for the pickets, and demanding that Blacks be employed, but without the sacking of Whites. Eventually Blumsteins conceded this demand.

In general, the party concentrated its anti-discrimination campaigns on unionised workplaces, where its 'shop units' could combine with outside protest to bring about change. In some cases, however — the Needle Trades and Transport Workers' unions, for instance — the party still had problems with its own members making concessions to racist workers.

The party clashed again with the Garveyites over the Italian invasion of Ethiopia in 1935. Initially they had attempted to work together to raise funds for the Ethiopians, but their fragile unity broke apart once the Garveyites started calling for a boycott of Harlem's Italian businessmen, particularly the ice-cream men. The Communist Party was able to take anti-fascist Italians to meetings of Blacks (and vice versa), and this helped reduce the possibility of conflict spreading to Harlem. The Party also played an important part in mobilising a massive anti-fascist march. The protest assembled in two places — one in the predominantly Italian part of Harlem, one in the mainly black area — and then combined in a

25,000-strong demonstration.

The second half of 1934 and most of 1935 represented the party's most successful period in Harlem. By August 1935 they had 700 black members in the section, and most had joined during that year.[42] There were a number of reasons for this growth.

This was a period when white workers could be won on occasions to fight against discrimination. 1934 was the year of the mass strikes in Minneapolis, Toledo and San Francisco, a general rise in militancy, and a growth of the AFL. There was another peak in class struggle from 1936-37, and this gave a massive boost to the non-racial, industrial unions of the Congress of Industrial Organizations (CIO). The party's black membership in Harlem reached its peak (1000 members) at the end of 1937.[43]

Another factor was probably important. The late 1920s and early 1930s saw the Comintern pursuing its ultra-sectarian 'third Period' policy of refusing to co-operate with reformists, who it denounced as 'social-fascists' and lumped with the Nazis. However after Hitler's triumph in Germany, this mad strategy began to break down, allowing the Communist Parties to engage in common action with reformists. For a brief period during 1934-5 the Communists in Harlem were able to participate in united action around specific issues.

Then the Seventh Congress of the Comintern, meeting in 1935, adopted a new strategy. As part of Stalin's policy of seeking an alliance with Britain and France against Nazi Germany, the Communist Parties were to seek alliances with the 'democratic' wing of the capitalist class. This 'Popular Front' went much further than the tactic put forward by Lenin and Trotsky of forming united fronts with reformists around specific issues. It amounted to subordinating the interests of the working class to a broad alliance with supposedly 'progressive' capitalists. In France and Spain the Popular Front strategy led to disastrous defeats. In the US it meant the Communist Party offered increasingly uncritical support for the Democratic Party, then in office under Franklin Roosevelt, and its allies in the trade union bureaucracy.

During the first part of the Popular Front period the total number of black members in Harlem was increasing. But the turnover was enormous. Between the spring of 1936 and the spring of 1938, the Communist Party in New York State recruited 2,320 Blacks and lost 1,518.[44] A qualitative change was under way: the party was losing working-class Blacks and recruiting from the middle classes, particularly intellectuals.

The party now began to argue for an 'American', non-violent path to socialism. More emphasis was placed on electoral work, and even the union activity became more electorally inclined. The old branches were closed down. Store-fronts were opened up to enable the people of Harlem to put their grievances to the Communists. Harlem became a division of the party and was reorganised according to electoral boundaries: a Lower Harlem section in an area inhabited mostly by Italians and Puerto Ricans: an Upper Harlem section which was mostly black; and a Washington Heights section, most of whose members were Irish or Jewish.[45] Political activity was reduced so that members could spend more time with their families or in leisure activities.

In 1938 activists were told not to direct the struggle of the unemployed against 'progressive officials supported by organised labour'. Progressive officials included Mayor LaGuardia and President Roosevelt.[46] Criticism of the CIO leadership declined. Attempts to secure alliances even led the party to play down the race issue. For instance, Communist organisers of the 1937 Jobs March to Washington failed to appoint black stewards and refused to appoint Blacks to delegations, for fear of alienating southern interests.[47]

Many of the best activists left the party. One wrote: 'Many of us ex-Reds saw the Communist Party become a recognised political party. We saw backward leaders join and ... turn the party from a deep red, to a pale pink, and finally a bright yellow.'[48] Naison summarises the situation:

> Harlem Communists found themselves on the defensive in confronting Harlem's economic problems. Weakened by defections of rank-and-file organisers, challenged by nationalists for leadership of Harlem's poor, the party experienced a narrowing of its local power base and growing skepticism of its political outlook ... the CIO's inaction against job discrimination, had shattered the confidence of many Harlemites in the power of inter-racial alliances to bring Blacks into the economic mainstream ... Communists tempered their advocacy of direct-action tactics and tried to insulate the unions from popular wrath ... Communists lost touch with the spirit of popular militancy in Harlem that their own activities had helped to inspire, and rekindled

deep fears of white treachery and betrayal.[49]

Even before the August 1939 Hitler-Stalin Pact Harlem's black Communists were in decline. The Pact itself had a devastating effect. The party had recruited many notable and influential black writers and musicians, mainly on the basis of fighting fascism. Now that party was condoning a pact with the arch-fascist. Many dropped away in disgust, leaving a demoralised shell.

In the early years the Communist Party in Harlem certainly made tactical mistakes. However they demonstrated one thing very clearly indeed: that it was possible for a largely white party to win credibility among Blacks to recruit black members and develop black leaders. Two factors made this possible: a clear commitment to working class Blacks and a rising level of class struggle. When the party deserted class struggle — under the impact of the Popular Front — it deserted the majority of Harlem's black population. This paved the way for the party's demise.

The failure of the Communist Party in areas like Harlem also had a longer-term effect. Many of the black activists and intellectuals who had been drawn towards the party, and who left it in disillusionment because of the Popular Front policy, concluded that Blacks could only further their cause on their own. The experience of the Communist Party in the 1930s, reflected in the fiction of black writers such as Ralph Ellison and Richard Wright, helped to turn a whole generation of Blacks against the idea of a non-racial revolutionary party uniting Blacks and Whites against both racism and capitalism. It was hardly surprising that black nationalism should be so strong when the struggle was revived by the next generation of Blacks.

The Civil Rights Movement

When the black struggle revived after the Second World War, its initial focus was in the South, where Blacks were still subject to the whole apparatus of formal and informal oppression erected in the 1870s. Jim Crow denied them even the formal rights to the vote and to equal treatment which bourgeois democracy generally offers its citizens.

By contrast the growing black working class of the northern cities enjoyed formal equality, but were still subject to institutionalised racism. The struggle to extend civil rights to Southern Blacks spilled over in the 1960s to the great northern ghettoes, sparking off a far more dangerous challenge to American capitalism.

Black American politics after 1945 can be roughly divided into three periods: militant, revolutionary, and reformist. The first period is that of the civil rights' movement, which sought the end of Jim Crow in the southern states. Although it has its antecedents in war-time protests, this movement really begins in 1955 with the Montgomery bus boycott. Its foremost leader was Martin Luther King, but his own organisation, the Southern Christian Leadership Conference (SCLC), was joined by others. Some, like the National Association for the Advancement of Coloured People were less radical. Others, such as the Student Non-violent Co-ordinating Committee (SNCC) and, to a lesser extent, the Congress on Racial Equality, were more so.

The second period began in 1964. Like the first, it was brought into being, not by politicians, but by mass action: the ghetto uprisings. The 'revolutionary' period is marked by the last years of Malcolm X, the call for 'Black Power', the Black Panthers, and in a different vein, the Dodge Revolutionary Union Movement (DRUM). The period closes with the collapse of the Panthers and DRUM, both in 1971.

The final period, the period of degeneration, is one of involvement in Democratic Party politics. It can be dated from 1972, when civil rights leaders, including Jesse Jackson, sponsored George McGovern's Presidential election campaign.

Montgomery's bus boycott was sparked by a single simple act by one black woman attempting to defend her dignity. Rosa Parks, tired from her day's work as a steamstress, was seated in the segrated section of a bus. It was the only place available. A white man demanded the seat. She refused. The police were called and she was arrested. It was not a planned defiance. It was just that Rosa Parks had had enough.

Her action acted as a catalyst. The overwhelming majority of the black residents of this Jim Crow southern city pledged themselves to boycott the buses until they had been desegregated. It was a hard battle and it was a long battle. Eventually, after twelve months, the Supreme Court found in their favour. By taking mass action the

40,000 black people of Montgomery achieved a famous victory.

Eight days after the Supreme Court judgement, a new wave of racist violence began. Racist gangs shot at buses. The Klan marched beneath burning crosses. One leader of the boycott had his home and church bombed. Another found sticks of dynamite outside his house.[50]

But this violence, and there was worse to come, could not hold back the movement for civil rights. All over the South Blacks fought for desegregation. 'Freedom rides' were organised on buses. Students occupied lunch-bar counters and refused to move until served or arrested. Racist chain stores were boycotted by northern customers in sympathy with the southern struggle. Voter registration drives were organised in the face of vicious intimidation. Then, in 1964, Congress passed the Civil Rights Act.

What was the social basis for this explosion of protest over civil rights?

Under the impact of the Second World War and then the post-war boom, there was a massive migration to the towns. In 1940, the black population of America was evenly divided between urban and rural areas. By 1960, almost three-quarters of all Blacks were urban residents. Over the same period the proportion of Blacks engaged in agriculture declined from 32 per cent to 8 per cent.[51]

The expansion of capitalism provided many new employment opportunities, but it was the Whites who got the better jobs and the Whites who got promoted. Urban life intensified the frustration of life under Jim Crow, but also created greater concentrations of black people, and the combination increased the possibilities of fighting back. The daily humiliation of segregation was an experience common to all Blacks, thus opening the door for a movement involving most classes of black people across the south.

However it was the educated black middle classes who took the initiative. They could sense the injustice of a system where their qualifications were worth less than those of white graduates. They could appreciate the hypocrisy of a society which, they were taught, was democratic, but where black people were prevented from voting. They also feared the boss less, because they were more likely to find employment.

At the meeting which launched the bus boycott there were, 'physicans, schoolteachers, lawyers, businessmen, postal workers, union leaders, and clergymen'.[52] No mention of the steamstress, the garbage collector, the domestic servant or the factory worker, although they were all involved in the boycott. In any case it was the clergymen who took the lead, to be followed, in time, by the students. The SNCC was originally launched as an organisation which could involve college students in mobilising poorer Blacks to register their votes.[53]

To say that the movement was led by middle-class Blacks is in no way to belittle its achievements. Nor is it to denigrate its leaders, most of whom were fine fighters, and very brave. This is especially true of Martin Luther King, a young Baptist minister who came to prominence through his leadership of the boycott. Religion provided a stimulus to King's activities. It also imposed a limitation: non-violence.

King's strategy amounted essentially to an alliance between the black middle class and the federal government. He aimed, by creating a political crisis in the South, to force Washington to intervene and impose desegration on racist Southern leaders such as Governor George Wallace of Alabama. The strategy worked. Successive presidents — Eisenhower, Kennedy and Johnson — sent federal troops and marshals to the South to enforce laws requiring equal treatment of Blacks. A succession of Supreme Court judgements, crowned by the Voting Rights Act of 1965, required the dismantling of the Jim Crow system.

The civil rights movement succeeded because the big corporations which dominated the federal government had no interest in perpetuating the antiquated system of forced labour and white terror to which Southern Blacks had been subject since Reconstruction. Faced with a swelling political crisis in the South, American capital was prepared to concede civil rights. Formal equality left intact the social and economic inequalities to which Northern Blacks were subject. In any case, the Jim Crow system increasingly didn't suit capitalist interests in the South itself, as agriculture declined in importance and Blacks were drawn to cities such as Atlanta to work in new industries.

As civil rights were gradually screwed out of the white supremacist states in the South, the focus of black activists began to shift towards the great northern ghettos.

The March on Washington in 1963 revealed some of the

weaknesses of the civil rights movement. It was called by the black trade union leader A Philip Randolph and backed by King and others. One leader of the SCLC predicted 'massive, militant, monumental sit-ins on Congress ... We will tie up public transportation by laying our bodies prostrate on runways of airports, across railroad tracks, and bus depots'. The NAACP, however, refused to add their support unless it was made clear that there would be no civil disobedience and unless the Kennedy administration was consulted about every stage of the march. King and Randolph agreed. Funds became available in abundance and Kennedy became most co-operative. As Manning Marable notes: 'The President came to understand that a symbolic protest would act as a necessary safety-valve for black discontent.'[54]

The radical wing of the civil rights movement either refused to participate or had their speeches censored. The march enabled the respectable elements (Randolph and the NAACP in particular) to place themselves at the head of the movement. In the end, a quarter of a million Americans came to a safety-valve, let off steam, and then went home. Malcolm X described the event as a 'one-day integrated picnic.'[55] Kennedy was able to make good use of the march. Not only was he able to persuade more backward democrats of the need to retreat, he also presented himself as a heroic man of the people. The following summer, according to Marable, King 'tried to halt desegregation demonstrations ... in a shabby effort not to embarrass Johnson during the presidential campaign.'[56]

King's politics had led him into alliances with the established black leadership, and through them into compromises with the liberal and, at that stage, dominant wing of capital.

Down below the revolt was just beginning. It has been estimated that in 1963, in eleven Southern states, there were 930 protest demonstrations in 115 cities. More than 20,000 people were arrested, compared to 3,600 in the period up to the end of 1961.[57] New forces were coming on to the streets. For the most part they were younger, more working-class and more unruly, with less to lose.

King could have embraced this new movement, but to do so would mean jettisoning his old base among middle-class Blacks (and a newly acquired base among middle-class Whites). It would also have meant breaking with pacifist politics. This he would not do. He stood still while the movement passed him by.

The nationalist politics of the Garvey movement failed to focus on any centres of power and foundered on its inability to deliver reforms. The non-violent direct action of the civil rights movement located the centres of power, secured some reforms, but foundered on its inability to deliver significant material improvements, particularly for poor Blacks in the North.

BLACK POWER 1: Uprisings

The closer the black movement drew to the North, the more likely it was to develop a revolutionary wing. Northern Blacks already had civil rights. Yet they occupied the lowest positions inside the working class of the big cities, doing the dirtiest jobs, earning the lowest pay, living in the worst housing. To improve their position would require a struggle against the very capitalists who had been prepared to lend support to the civil rights movement in the South. As Northern Blacks took to the streets, they posed a revolutionary challenge to the capitalist system.

One writer has described the mood of Detroit in 1964 as one of 'black discontent and white optimism'[58] For Detroit, so for most of America, or at least its northern and west coast cities. In the summer of 1964 there were riots in Harlem. Black discontent deepened and white optimism began to evaporate. The level of black resistance increased; the riots became uprisings. In 1965 there were nine, 38 in 1966, 128 in 1967, and 131 in the first six months of 1968.[59]

An explanation for this changed mood cannot be found in terms of rising levels of unemployment. Official statistics suggest that non-white unemployment fell from 10.8 per cent in 1963 to 6.7 per cent in 1968.[60] But the mid-1960s was a period of rising expectations. This had been created by the expansion of capitalism, but it had been intensified by the achievements of the civil rights movement. Despite the promises on equality Blacks were still getting a raw deal. When they got jobs it was normally the 'shit jobs'. By the 1960s 70 per cent of all employed black people were in unskilled and semi-skilled blue-collar and service jobs.[61] In 1963, white male income averaged $1,365 more than that of similarly educated black men.[62] On average Whites were paid almost twice as much as Blacks.[63] Unemployment rates for Blacks remained more than twice those for Whites.[64]

In a land of expanding opportunities a generation of black

working class youth felt trapped in the ghetto, impoverished and subject to continuing harassment by racist police. Some Blacks, a minority, had benefited from the 'second reconstruction', but not they. In Watts, scene of one of the most violent uprisings, 34 per cent of adult Blacks were unemployed, and the figure was twice this high among teenagers. More than 60 per cent of the people in the area existed on welfare or relief payments.[65]

The uprisings were not a simple expression of 'black anger', they were a revolt by *working class Blacks*. As Philip Foner states: 'By the summer of 1965, the mass of Blacks living in the Northern ghettoes were keenly aware that civil rights victories benefited primarily a very small percentage of middle-class Blacks, while their own predicament remained the same or worsened.'[66]

The Watts uprising of 1965 covered a 50-square mile area of Los Angeles. It ended with 34 deaths, mostly Blacks killed by police or National Guardsmen. During the disturbances, which lasted for six whole days, 4,200 people were arrested and 600 buildings damaged or destroyed, at a cost of at least $100 million. One journalist reported that 7,000 people were involved during the second night, and another estimated that altogether up to 65,000 were involved.[67] Another report said that 15 per cent of the population were actively involved, and that another 35-40 per cent were 'active spectators.'[68]

The Detroit uprising of 1967 was on an even larger scale: 5,000 people were left homeless, 1,300 buildings destroyed, 2,700 buildings looted, and the total cost was calculated at $500 million. 3,800 people were arrested, 347 were injured and 43 died (nine white and 34 black). 'A four-year old girl was killed when a tank sprayed the room she was in because someone lit a cigarette and spooked the guardsmen.' This time a regiment of 'paras' fresh from Vietnam joined the other forces of the state to put down the uprising.[69]

These uprisings not only had a black nationalist dynamic (Blacks versus 'White' state), they also had a class dynamic. The civil rights struggle could unite all classes against discrimination. This new, 'revolutionary' struggle was against poverty, unemployment, rotten jobs and police brutality. Those were not the concerns of the middle classes and it was not they who did the fighting.

According to Foner: 'When the activists came north to aid in the struggle for housing, education and jobs, they met black people in the ghettoes who knew from bitter experience that white racists in the police force laughed at non-violence and respected only effective self-defence.'[70] The following is one account of a meeting addressed by Martin Luther King in Watts, just after the uprising had come to an end:

> ... he spoke to an overflow crowd ... he was heckled, jeered and rejected. The Northern ghetto Negro was showing a readiness to fight for more than the right to vote.
>
> 'All over America,' Dr King said, 'the Negroes must join hands —'
> 'And burn!' interrupted a man standing on the edge of the crowd.
> A woman told Dr King, 'Let Chief Parker and Mayor Yorty come down here and see how we live.'
> Dr King promised to try to get Chief Parker and Mayor Yorty down to Watts. 'I know you'll be courteous to them,' he said. The crowd roared with laughter ... The Watts rebels were looking for new leaders.[71]

New leaders, new heroes and new politics ... a new movement. This new movement acquired a name: Black Power.

'Black Power' is more a description of a mood — of anger, some confidence and a desire for change — than of a distinct ideology. The slogan was first used by Stokely Carmichael on a voters' registration march through Mississippi in June 1966. It represented for him, and for the leadership of the SNCC, a break from militant 'integrationism'. To the more conservative black leaders and to most Whites it sounded threatening. It was for this very reason that it became popular among the younger, more radical Blacks. According to Foner, 'The fact that the "Black Power" slogan struck fear into the white community proved to the black masses that it was more effective than "Freedom Now".'[72]

For those wishing to identify with a struggle more militant than the non-violence of the civil rights movement, 'Black Power' was a valuable statement. It fitted the mood of the ghetto uprisings. One psychologist summed up the attitude of the participants in the Watts Uprising as: 'It is better to be feared, than to be treated with contempt'.[73]

In the book titled **Black Power** Stokely Carmichael and Charles Hamilton argued that black people in America should form a colony, and 'stand as colonial subjects in relation to the white society'.[74] For them, the task was to unite black people against the 'white power structure'. However, their view of this 'white power structure' was vague; the notion of 'white society' was confused; the precise content of 'Black Power' remained obscure.[75] Carmichael eventually departed for Africa, where he lived under his adopted name, Kwame Ture.

The hero of 'Black Power' was a man who had been assassinated before the concept had been invented. He was Malcolm X.

2: Malcolm X

It is usually argued that there are two main traditions in Black American politics: integrationist and separatist.[76] The integrationists, including the NAACP but also Martin Luther King, aimed at racial equality within a reformed but essentially capitalist America. The separatists believed that this only increased subservience to the Whites. Instead they encouraged black business, religious and political organisation separated from, but existing alongside, white (capitalist) institutions. Their hero was Marcus Garvey. Malcolm X came from the separatist tradition, but under the impact of struggle attempted to synthesise the best of both traditions into a new and revolutionary politics.

Malcolm was born in 1925. When he was still young, his father, a Garveyite Baptist minister, was murdered by racists. His mother was driven to insanity by the appalling conditions she was forced to endure. At an early age Malcolm moved to Detroit, then later to Harlem. He became a hustler before turning to more serious criminal activity. Caught, he was sent to prison, where he stayed for seven years.

While in prison Malcolm was persuaded to join the Nation of Islam by its founder and leader, the Honorable Elijah Muhammad. The Nation of Islam was a separatist sect *par excellence*. It even rejected the white man's god. It was, however, an all-American creation, and did not follow orthodox Islamic doctrine. Its followers became known as Black Muslims. Eventually it made Elijah Muhammad one of the wealthiest men in America. Soon after his parole, in 1952, Malcolm became a Black Muslim minister. In 1963, he was appointed its national minister.

Malcolm was instrumental in the rapid growth of the Black Muslims in the late 1950s and early 1960s. But by 1961 dissatisfaction was beginning to take root. Reflecting on this period in his **Autobiography** he comments:

... privately I was convinced that our nation of Islam could be an even greater force in the American Black man's overall struggle — if we engaged in more *action*. By that, I mean I thought privately that we should have amended, or relaxed, our general non-engagement policy. I felt that, wherever black people committed themselves, in the Little Rocks and the Birminghams and other places, militantly disciplined Muslims should also be there — for all the world to see, and respect, and discuss.[77]

Following the assassination of President Kennedy in 1962, Malcolm said he thought the chickens had come home to roost; meaning that Kennedy had been a victim of the hate and violence of a society of which he was the favourite son. Malcolm added, although his **Autobiography** misses this from his account: 'Being a farm boy myself, chickens coming home to roost never did make me sad; they've always made me glad'.[78] For this he was suspended by Elijah Muhammad. Before the suspension could be extended Malcolm resigned. It was not an easy decision to become an 'independent leader', but, he says: 'In the end, I reasoned that the decision had been made for me. The ghetto masses already had entrusted me with an image of leadership among them.'[79]

> I knew that the great lack of most of the big-named 'Negro leaders' was their lack of any true rapport with the ghetto Negroes. How could they have any true rapport when they spent most of their time 'integrating' with white people? I knew that the ghetto people knew that I never left the ghetto in spirit, and I never left it physically any more than I had to. I had a ghetto instinct; for instance, I could feel if tension was beyond normal in a ghetto audience ...
>
> I could talk over the ABC, CBS or NBC microphones, at Harvard or Tuskegee; I could talk with the so-called 'middle-class' Negro and with the ghetto blacks (whom all the other leaders just talked *about*).[80]

Soon after the split Malcolm X made a pilgrimage to Mecca and travelled to West Africa. He was treated almost as if he were *the* leader of Black America. He had meetings with Prince Faisal of Saudi Arabia and Kwame Nkrumah, President of Ghana and on a later visit with Presidents Nasser of Egypt, Azikwe of Nigeria, Sekou Touré of Guinea, Kenyatta of Kenya and Obote of Uganda. This improved his standing as a black leader in America and also influenced the direction of his politics. In June 1964, following his return from Mecca, he formed a new organisation, the Organisation of Afro-American Unity. At this stage, and at the time of his assassination in

February 1965,[81] his ideas were still developing.

Malcolm rejected his old separatist attitude towards Whites. 'In the past, yes, I have made sweeping indictments of all white people', he admitted, 'I never will be guilty of that again — as I know now that some white people are truly sincere, that some truly are capable of being brotherly toward a black man.' However, he excluded Whites from his new organisation. 'Even the best white members', he argued, 'will slow down the Negroes' discovery of what they need to do, and particularly of what they can do — for themselves, working by themselves.' He added: 'I have these very deep feelings that white people who want to join black organisations are really just taking the escapist way to salve their consciences'. He advised 'sincere white people' to 'work in conjunction with us — each of us working among our own kind'.[82]

He began to believe that 'the white man is not inherently evil, but America's society influences him to act evilly.'[83] He began to identify 'America's society' with 'capitalism', and he began to argue in favour of 'socialism' and 'revolution'. However his understanding of these concepts was hazy. He equated 'socialism' with most of the African states:

> ... all of the countries that are emerging today from under the shackles of colonialism are turning toward socialism. I don't think it's an accident. Most of the countries that were colonial powers were capitalist countries, and the last bulwark of capitalism today is America. It's impossible for a white person to believe in capitalism and not believe in racism. You can't have capitalism without racism. And if you find one and you happen to get that person into a conversation and they have a philosophy that makes you sure they don't have this racism in their outlook, usually they're socialists or their political philosophy is socialism.[84]

Three days before he was murdered, Malcolm expressed himself more clearly than he had done before. In his last formal speech he argued:

> We are living in an era of revolution, and the revolt of the American Negro is part of the rebellion against the oppression and colonialism which has characterised this era ... It is incorrect to classify the revolt of the negro as simply a racial conflict of black against white, or as a purely American problem. Rather, we are today seeing a global rebellion of the oppressed against the oppressor, the exploited against

the exploiter.[85]

The American Socialist Workers Party (which is not connected with the British SWP) claimed that, at his death, Malcolm X was moving towards adopting a revolutionary socialist position. This is unlikely. He still described himself as a nationalist. Furthermore, his attitude towards regimes such as those in Egypt and Ghana, not to mention Kenya and Nigeria, shows that he had not yet accepted that the working class is central to any real socialist change in society. Whether they liked it or not, all these regimes were forced to accept the priorities of a world capitalist system, and all were involved in suppressing revolts by workers.

One might argue that, as with Garvey, Malcolm turned to Africa for inspiration, because, in the mid-1960s, the white working class in the US looked so unattractive. Perhaps in the early 1970s, with the African situation a little clearer and the American working class beginning to stir, he might have reviewed his position. Perhaps. But much happened in between ...

Malcolm X was not a Marxist, and he was not attempting to build a party on the basis of Leninist principles. He is still a man to be greatly admired. He was a nationalist, but had broken from the Garvey mould. He rejected the American state and its racist supporters and was prepared to fight. He inspired a generation to take up the struggle against the American beast. He achieved this through his simple commitment to defend those Blacks who defended themselves 'by any means necessary'.

3: The Black Panthers

The Black Panthers were formed by Huey P Newton and Bobby Seale in 1966. Later others joined the leadership, including Eldridge Cleaver. By 1968 they had become a major national organisation, widely respected by black Americans. The Panthers attempted to provide a leadership for the generation of black youth that had been radicalised by the ghetto uprisings.

The hallmark of the Black Panther Party in its early days was its emphasis on armed self-defence. Their attitude has been summarised by one writer as 'If the police patrolled the community, you patrolled the police. If they pulled a gun on you, you pulled a gun on them — in self-defence.'[86] Initially the organisation was called the Black Panther Party for Self-Defence, and Newton was described as the Minister of

Defence. Their emphasis on arms provided them with notoriety in the media, and recruits in the ghettoes.

The Panthers endeavoured to give some content to the notion of 'Black Power'. They attempted to build on the politics of Malcolm X, but were also influenced by Fanon, Mao and Che Guevara. They rejected the retreat to cultural nationalism, with its emphasis on African hairstyles, African clothes, everything African — and argued instead for revolutionary nationalism. Arms were intended for immediate defence and ultimate liberation.

Cleaver recounted his first meeting with the Panthers, a gathering to discuss a memorial rally for Malcolm X in 1967:

> 'OK,' said Ballard [a cultural nationalist]. 'We have the program broken down into subjects: Politics, Economics, Self-Defence and Black Culture. Now which section do you brothers want to speak under?' This was the sort of question which in my experience had always signalled the beginning of a two-hour debate with this group. 'It doesn't matter what section we speak under,' Huey said. 'Our message is one and the same. We're going to talk about black people arming themselves in a political fashion to exert organised force in the political arena to see to it that their desires and needs are met. Otherwise there will be a political consequence. And the only culture worth talking about is revolutionary culture. So it doesn't matter what heading you put on it, we're going to talk about political power growing out of the barrel of a gun.'
>
> 'OK,' Roy Ballard said. He paused, then added, 'Let's put it under Politics.'[87]

Although the Panthers accepted Carmichael's argument that Blacks were a colonised people, they saw 'white society' as a 'class society'. The enemy was capitalism, not the whole white population. It was therefore possible to envisage oppressed Whites joining forces with oppressed Blacks. Cleaver once prophesied:

> Not just a race war, which in itself would destroy this country, but a guerilla resistance movement that will amount to a second civil war, with thousands of white John Browns fighting on the side of the Blacks, plunging America into the depths of its most desperate nightmare.[88]

The Panthers' analysis encouraged them to look for white allies. It also fostered a sceptical view of the black bourgeoisie. However, their appreciation of 'class' was vague, and, in practice, they tended to consider that the main cleavage was between capitalism and the black community. This inhibited them from understanding that, at least in the long term, they needed to look to the working class, black and white, if they were to defeat capitalism.

They built their base among 'the brothers on the block'. That is, the unemployed and *lumpen*, mainly male youth, who had been at the centre of the uprisings. These angry young men usually had time on their hands to engage in Party activity. In **Seize the Time**, Bobby Seale argued:

> The youth are a vast reservoir of revolutionary potential. The lumpen proletarian brothers on the block, and sisters, and everybody in the streets who are trying to make it, are part of this reservoir which one day will come forth like a wild, rushing stream.[89]

The Panthers' orientation on the *lumpenproletariat* of the black ghettos was responsible both for their success in building a mass organisation, and for their ultimate demise. The situation of unemployed ghetto youth, dependent on welfare payments, casual work, and sometimes petty crime, does not encourage them to engage in collective action. Indeed, one of the worst aspects of black oppression lies in the way that the poverty of the ghetto drives black people to compete with each other, the poor often robbing the poor. By comparison, the situation of the *proletariat* drives them towards collective action and organisation. The workplace breeds solidarity, the ghetto mutual distrust.

when workers unite against the boss, they fight for themselves, disciplined by the collective exploitation they suffer at work. But the *lumpenproletariat* can act as a cohesive force only when discipline is imposed *from without*. The Panthers had to argue with the 'brothers on the block' not to fight for themselves, but to *serve* the community. The Panthers' politics of service, based on a moral appeal to ghetto youth, arose from the economic position of the 'brothers on the block'.

Service entailed two elements. Firstly, and initially of greatest importance, was 'patrolling the pigs'. Secondly, and of increasing importance, was involvement in various 'survival programmes'. 'Breakfast for children' was the most famous, but also free buses to prisons, free clothing, free plumbing and so on. Huey Newton argued that these two forms of activity were complementary, and both were aimed at assisting the Panthers to build a base for their politics.

In practice the two forms of activity had different dynamics. 'Patrolling the pigs' entailed confrontation with the state, and tended towards revolutionary politics, albeit in an adventurist form. The 'survival programmes' tended towards do-it-yourself reformism, militant charity work which could avoid confrontation.

These two kinds of activity *directly* related to different sections of the ghetto poor. Indirectly, they related to the different class forces present within the ghetto. The proletariat has an unequivocal interest in the overthrow of capitalism, in the socialist revolution, which necessarily bases itself on workers' power. The petty bourgeoisie, on the other hand, sandwiched between the two major classes, has a tendency to vacillate and to look for compromise.

In attempting to serve the 'community' the Panthers were attempting to serve different class forces with different class interests: revolution and reform. The Panthers were being pulled by two horses, by two dynamics. At first, this was manageable. With a high level of struggle and a mood of optimism the horses at least pulled in the same direction, even if at different speeds. As the mass movement subsided the horses began to pull in different directions, and eventually they pulled the Panthers apart.

The ambiguity, although not apparent, was actually present in the Panthers' founding statement, their Ten Point Programme.[90] Point Two, for instance, stated: 'We want full employment for our people'. In practice this could be, and was, interpreted as a call to create jobs in the ghetto by establishing co-operatives. Newton later argued that because revolution was a 'process', their programme was 'open-ended', and aimed only at taking people to a 'higher level'. Unfortunately the politics of the Panthers did not evolve sufficiently to find that 'higher level'. They became beset by problems which, in the main, were products of their politics.

These problems were intensified by the nature of their base. Laurie and Sy Landy argued in an article for **International Socialism**:

> Marx pointed out ... that the *lumpen proletariat* cannot be organised democratically except as adjuncts of a larger proletarian movement. The leader who organises a *lumpen proletariat* base may succeed if he allows it to act in as volatile a fashion as it wishes to; but should he try to check its actions, then his base will vanish. This was the dilemma continually confronting the Black Panther party.[91]

The leadership of the Panthers attempted to overcome the

tensions in their organisation by means of discipline and education. They passed a series of rules[92] and enforced them by suspension and expulsion. The rules laid down, for instance, that members must not be drunk or 'high' while carrying arms. They also made it mandatory for members to attend political education classes and for the leadership to read for at least two hours a day. Discipline and education are necessary in any political organisation, but they cannot be a substitute for agreement on the general direction of the organisation.

Many of the Panthers' supporters were happy to carry a gun; it helped to give them pride in themselves by making them feel important. But the same people often had little interest in changing direction to a more 'political' and less militaristic approach. The very nature of their existence — fighting for survival on the edge of legality — did nothing to encourage an understanding of the need for a longer term approach. Newton understood the need for serious political study, for shifts in strategy, for tactical flexibility, but in this he was at odds with the material circumstances of his supporters. Moreover, his conception of revolutionary politics was shaped by Stalinism in its various forms — Russia, Cuba, China — rather than by classical Marxism with its orientation on the industrial working class.

Given the emphasis on guns and the talk of revolution it was inevitable that the Panthers would attract the active opposition of the state. Sometimes they seemed surprised that the 'pigs' played dirty. The Panthers were subjected to continual surveillance and raids on their offices. Newton spent thirty-three months in prison, before the police eventually dropped the charges. Cleaver was forced into exile. Many Panthers were assassinated by the police, including Fred Hampton and Bobby Hutton from the leadership.

As an elite arms-bearing force, they gained much respect. But respect is not the same as active solidarity. When they were attacked by the state they were incapable of mounting the kind of campaign that was necessary to defend themselves. Had the Panthers concentrated on building support for revolutionary politics in the workplaces there would have been a possibility that workers might use their economic power to defend them. In part this problem was later recognised by Newton. In **Revolutionary Suicide**, published in 1973, he wrote:

We sought to provide a counter-force, a positive image of strong and unafraid Black men in the community. The emphasis on weapons was a necessary phase in our evolution, based on Frantz Fanon's contention that the people have to be shown that the colonisers and their agents — the police — are not bullet-proof. We saw this action as a bold step in making our programme known and raising the consciousness of the people.

But we soon discovered that weapons and uniforms set us apart from the community. We were looked upon as an *ad hoc* military group, acting outside the community fabric and too radical to be a part of it. Perhaps some of our tactics at the time were extreme; perhaps we placed too much emphasis on military action. We saw ourselves as the revolutionary 'vanguard' and did not fully understand then that only the people can create the revolution.[93]

Physical suppression was not, however, the only problem the Panthers faced. Many of their allies proved unreliable. This was particularly true of the black businessmen whose assistance was required if the 'survival programmes' were to succeed. Sufficient financial and material support failed to appear.

The Panthers were also unfortunate in their choice of white allies. This was the period of the anti-Vietnam War movement, and they turned to some of its most prominent activist groups. These included the Peace and Freedom Party and the political fringe of the hippy movement, the Yippies led by Jerry Rubin. There was also the White Panther Party. Their first demand was 'Full endorsement and support of the Black Panther Party's 10 point program and platform'. The second demand was 'Total assault on the culture by any means necessary, including rock and roll, dope, and fucking in the streets.'[94] They also identified with Maoists and with a terrorist group, the Weathermen. It was because the Panthers lacked an understanding of the need to relate to the working class that they allied themselves with these colourful, but useless, organisations.

Under pressure the Panthers moved in a number of directions. They stood in elections to bourgeois institutions; not as a platform for revolutionary ideas, but to increase 'community control.' They proposed an anti-fascist alliance, which would include Democrats and even Republicans. They moved into alliances with the Communist Party. None of these avenues provided a way out of their difficulties.

Eventually they split. Cleaver, who particularly disliked

involvement with the Communist Party, charged Newton with 'revisionism'. Newton characterised Cleaver's opposition as 'adventurist'.[95] Newton later said of Cleaver that his 'ideology was based on the rhetoric of violence; his speeches abounded in either/or absolutes, like "Either you pick up that gun or remain a snivelling coward".'[96]

This was the tragic end to a movement which mobilised thousands of black youth in a revolutionary struggle against capitalism and the American state. The Panthers have left us an important lesson in revolutionary politics. No matter how brave, how determined, how hard you fight, you do not always win. You need a mass movement and you need correct politics. Those politics need to place the working class, not the ghetto youth, at the centre of the struggle.

4: DRUM

The new mood of the late 1960s was infectious, and black workers brought a new militancy to their workplaces and unions. There was a Black Panther caucus in the General Motors plant in Freemont, California. At the Ford plant in Mahwah, New Jersey, the United Black Brotherhood organised a wildcat unofficial strike lasting three days. In the Chicago Transit Company there was a black-led, white-supported, strike against the racist leadership of the Local (union branch).[97]

The formation in mid-1968 of the Dodge Revolutionary Union Movement (DRUM) by a group of socialist militants, was particularly significant. DRUM was the product of a particular set of circumstances in the Detroit Area in 1968. By that stage the City's black population had grown to 40 per cent of the total.[98] In the Detroit area one auto worker in four was black, nearly twice the national average. The big three car companies — General Motors, Ford and Chrysler — expanded production during most of the 1960s, and increased their combined workforce by over 30 percent.[99] In Detroit most of the new workers were young. A large proportion were also black.[100]

However, Blacks were excluded from the better jobs and were pushed into the dirtiest, noisiest, most gruelling, most dangerous work: the foundry, the body shop and engine assembly. Chrysler's Dodge Main plant was typical. The majority of the workers were black, but 99 per cent of all general foremen were white, 95 per cent of foremen were white, all the superintendents were white, 90 per cent of skilled tradesmen were white, and 90 per cent of skilled apprentices were white.[101]

The United Auto Workers (UAW), virtually the only union in the auto industry, was according to the NAACP 'the best of the industrial unions on the issue of race'.[102] This flattering view was not shared by black militants in the industry. They pointed to the fact that there was only one black American on the union's 26-person Executive Board; and he had denounced those involved in the Detroit Uprising as 'hoodlums and hatemongers'.[103]

The Detroit Uprising had occurred less than one year before the formation of DRUM. It has been described by some as 'The Great Rebellion' and by others as an 'insurrection'. It increased racial awareness and inspired new confidence, particularly among young blacks. One side-effect of the uprising was that it encouraged the car companies to take on a larger number of the unemployed black youth.

So the situation in the Detroit motor industry was explosive, with a concentration of young black workers radicalised by the huge uprising and politicised by prejudice. DRUM provided a conscious expression of their grievances and an organisation for their anger.

DRUM inspired other Revolutionary Union Movements, and early in 1969 the League of Revolutionary Black Workers was formed to co-ordinate their activities. It had a seven-man executive committee. Four of them had been members of a group which met to read Marx's **Capital**: John Watson, General Baker, Luke Tripp and John Williams. They had also participated in a variety of radical black organisations, and Watson, at least, had attended some meetings of the American Socialist Workers Party.

Watson edited the League's paper the **Inner-City Voice,** which was launched in September 1967, and had a print run of about 10,000. He was a semi-permanent student, and in the academic year 1968-1969 was elected to edit the Wayne State University paper, **South End**. It was printed daily and had a run of 18,000. Watson had worked for a while on the **Detroit News**, the City's largest selling paper. There he met two others who were to join the executive: Mike Hamlin, a truck driver, and Ken Cockrel, a law student, who was working as his assistant.[104] The seventh executive member Chuck Wooten, worked with General Baker at Dodge Main.

This group was influenced by a variety of political ideas: from Malcolm X, Che, Fanon, Lenin, Mao, C L R James and others. Later they were to polarise into two main groups. Watson, Hamlin and Cockrel tended to emphasise class politics. The others were pulled more by nationalist arguments. Tripp and Williams envisaged a black-led socialist revolution that would culminate in separate black and white socialist states.[105] Despite their heterogeneity, the whole leadership of the League shared an understanding of the centrality of the black working class in the revolutionary process.

The masthead of **South End** proclaimed 'One class conscious worker is worth 100 students.'[106] Watson explained their poisition: 'Our analysis tells us that the basic power of black people lies at the point of production, that the basic power we have is the power as workers.' Elsewhere he said:

> In one factory we have 10,000 people who are faced with the same brutal conditions ... When you go out into the community, the interests of the people ... are going to be much more dispersed ... Just in terms of expediency there are greater possiblities in the organisation of the plant ... The kinds of actions which can be taken [in the community] are not as effectively damaging to the ruling class as the kinds of actions which can be taken in the plant ... When you close down Hamtrack assembly plant ... for a day you can cost Chrysler corporation 1000 cars.[107]

The group saw their task in an international context. 'If the Black Revolution can overthrow capitalism and imperialism in the US, then the whole world will be freed ... With this understanding, let us praise the Vietnamese and Koreans, but let us pass the ammunition and do our own thing.'[108] Watson clarified their argument against capitalism:

> We are no more for integrated capitalism than for segregated capitalism. Neither are we in favor of a separate state, based on the same class lines as this society. We are against a separate state in which a black capitalist class exploits a black proletariat. We are opposed also to all sorts of haphazard talk which doesn't tell us what to do in the United States ... We have studied the history of the Russian Bolsheviks and found a specific pamphlet by Lenin called **Where to begin**, written in 1903, before he wrote **What is to be done?** where he described the role a newspaper could play. A newspaper was the focus

of a permanent organisation. It could provide a bridge between the peaks of activity ... It creates the kind of division of labor needed not just for the newspaper but for a revolutionary organisation.[109]

Although the group sympathised with the revolutionary politics of the Black Panthers they disagreed with their emphasis on the *lumpen proletariat.* They rejected too the Panthers' approach of appearing as 'superheroes' who the masses 'might admire but would be afraid to imitate'. Cockrel once said that none of the League's supporters had been killed by the police or sentenced to jail, and indicated that this was because they employed tactics very different to those of the Panthers.

On 2 May 1968, 4000 workers at Dodge Main joined the first wildcat strike to hit the plant for fourteen years. The main reason was a speed-up from 49 to 58 units per hour. When the workers returned to work after the strike, management sacked seven 'leaders': five black men and two white women. Although most of the participants had been white, Blacks bore the brunt of the attack. Eventually management reinstated five of the seven, but General Baker and another black man remained sacked. The UAW refused to act. It was then that Baker called together some readers of the **Inner City Voice**, which was being sold at the gates, and formed DRUM.

DRUM started to produce a regular factory bulletin. It took up issues such as the accountability of UAW officials, discriminatory hiring and unsafe machinery. The ninth bulletin demanded increased employment of Blacks at various levels and in various types of work. It also demanded equal pay for black workers in Chrysler South Africa and reinstatement of the sacked workers. Another demand was for the black members to cease paying their dues to the union, and for the funds to be redirected to the black community. With the exception of this last demand, their agitation was well received by black workers.

Next they called a boycott of two local bars which refused to hire Blacks. They achieved 95 per cent co-operation from workers at the plant and won their demands. This boosted their confidence. On 7 July they called a wildcat. Picket lines were manned by black students, unemployed youth and other 'community people', in order to protect the jobs of auto workers; 70 per cent of the black workers stayed out. Whites were not asked to join the stoppage, but some did so nevertheless. The wildcat lasted two days. Although DRUM did not win its demands it was encouraged by the support. The strike had stopped the production of about 1,900 cars.[110]

DRUM maintained its activity with rallies, marches, parties and raffles. According to one source they had 700 dues-paying members and held weekly meetings attended by 400 workers.[111] They rapidly inspired imitators. The most important was the Eldon Avenue Revolutionary Union Movement (ELRUM) based at Chrsyler's gear and axle plant. There was also FRUM at Ford's River Rouge complex, CADRUM at Cadillac's Fleetwood factory and so on. There were RUMs in other industries and in other cities.

Another wildcat was called by ELRUM in January 1969. Production was totally halted, partly because Blacks comprised a larger proportion of the workforce. As with the DRUM wildcat no auto workers appeared on the picket line. Despite this 26 workers were fired. Most of them were ELRUM activists and this had a devastating effect on their ability to organise in the plant.The League later evaluated the strike as 'premature'. The real problem was that if they were to defend themselves from such attacks they needed support from white workers as well as black.

DRUM also participated in union elections. In 1968 they stood Ron March for the trusteeship of Local 3. In the first round he won the highest vote, but in the run-off he was defeated by 2,091 to 1,386. DRUM argued that the defeat had occurred because of a threat by Chrysler to move the plant if March won, because of police intimidation, and because of the votes of 1,300 retired white workers. All these were factors and DRUM could claim a moral victory. However, when DRUM stood candidates in subsequent elections they were also unsuccessful, except when they stood in an alliance with others. Although Blacks were a majority in plants such as Dodge Main and Eldon Avenue, militant Blacks were a minority and so needed an alliance either with more moderate Blacks or with white militants.

DRUM, ELRUM and the others had an active life span of only about two years. But they made an impact because they related to genuine grievances and were able to mobilise a substantial number of workers for strike action. Moderate black leaders in the union were forced to demand more Blacks in leading positions. Foner notes that 'suddenly the UAW leadership stopped the practice of mobilising opposition to black candidates in local elections,' and as a result

Blacks were successfully elected in many Locals.[112] The union discovered (if they did not know it already) that Blacks as such were not the problem, it was angry and organised Blacks that they needed to block.[113] It is possible that DRUM even made an impact on the hiring policies of some of the companies; there was certainly a rapid increase in the number of black foremen.[114]

Concessions of this kind probably helped to undercut the League's appeal. However, the League had other, more fundamental problems. There was a slump in the car industry beginning in July 1969 and lay-offs followed. DRUM's base among young black workers was hit particularly hard because of the seniority agreements. Chuck Wooten was among a number of militants to be victimised. Meanwhile, the general mood of ghetto resistance also had begun to wane.

On 12 June 1971, Watson, Cockrel and Hamlin resigned from the League. The immediate causes of the split were twofold. The Watson group, and to some extent Tripp and Williams, had seen the 'in-plant' organising of DRUM and the other groups as one component of a broader revolutionary movement. Consequently they put resources into opening a bookstore, establishing a bookclub, publishing, making a film, and organising community and student groups. They also became involved in the Black Workers Congress, a national or potentially national organisation. General Baker, in particular, was opposed to these developments, arguing that the decline in 'in-plant' organisation had occurred because resources had been squandered; that they had moved too far too fast.

Eventually the Watson group issued an ultimatum. They demanded an education programme aimed at 'losing' some of the more backward members who they considered to be a block on the development of the group. They were opposed to attacks on comrades who lived with white women and to criticism of Marx as a mere 'honkie'.[115] Hamlin later argued:

> We had no meaningful political education program. We tried it a number of times but it was sabotaged by the attitude of reactionary nationalists. They didn't want to study Marxism so they used various tactics to stop the classes. That is not to say that some of our instructors were not dull for workers, but that's another question. The nationalists would say that Marx and Lenin were white and not relevant.[116]

Hamlin points to a shortcoming in the League's politics which led to a major weakness. The League focussed on the struggles in the car plants and recruited the most militant black workers. It was right to do this. Any revolutionary organisation which fails to involve itself in the struggles of workers will degenerate into a sterile sect. But those organisations which relate *only* to workplace militancy tend to be highly unstable — they go up and down with the struggle. A revolutionary socialist party doesn't simply relate to struggles; it seeks to win individuals to revolutionary socialist *ideas*. These individuals might not be workers; they might be students or even petty bourgeois. They are nevertheless important — because they bring stability, and organisational and intellectual skills, to a party of revolutionary workers.

The Black Workers Congress had its own problems, some of them created by James Forman, the organisation's executive secretary.[117] Watson dropped out to complete his studies. Cockrel dropped out to concentrate on law and electoral politics. Hamlin and the remains of the Black Workers Congress ended up participating in discussions with a number of Maoists. The Baker group kept the League alive for a while. He opened a China-Albania Bookstore, and eventually joined another Maoist group, the Communist League.

The tragedy of the League's demise was underlined by the upsurge in struggle which occurred in 1973. This involved black and white workers, and wildcats shut down three Chrysler plants: Jefferson Assembly, Mack Stamping and Detroit Forge. The Jefferson dispute was particularly dramatic. Two black militants took control of the electric control cage, and by pushing one button they stopped the whole line. They demanded the removal of a white supervisor who had been harassing them. Workers — Black, White and Arab — gathered round the cage with chains in hand, and thirteen hours later management backed down.

The upsurge of 1973 showed that even white workers, many of whom accepted racist ideas, would not tolerate management's attacks on working conditions forever. It provided examples of black workers leading white workers in struggle. Unfortunately the League was not around to strengthen and politicise these strikes. The League had had hundreds of revolutionary supporters in the Detroit car plants. Politically trained, organised, and relating to white workers, they could perhaps have transformed these struggles.

The League had made mistakes in relating to the older and more backward black workers: the tone of its leaflets had been too shrill; it had disrupted union meetings; it had argued that Blacks should be allowed to withdraw from the union. But it made a more fundamental mistake. It effectively wrote off the whole of the white workforce.

One white auto worker, a member of the International Socialists (US), commented:

> The weakness of DRUM ... derived in the main from the prejudices of white workers, but DRUM can be faulted for paying insufficient attention to overcoming the racism of white workers and for not distinguishing between the union leadership and the union itself. This made it easier for the leadership to isolate them, to brand them as splitters and to win the compliance of other workers in their victimisation.[118]

Goergakas and Surkin, in their book on the League, note that some white workers could display greater militancy than some black workers. They mention the 4000 skilled workers at the General Motors Technical Centre who formed barricades during the 1970 strike.[119] In the same year there was a marvellous wildcat at Eldon Avenue in opposition to the victimisation of a black worker, John Scott. 'It had an old-fashioned unity — young and old, black and white, men and women.'[120]

There were individual militants that League members could have worked with. Most significantly there was the rank and file United National Caucus led by Pete Kelly from the Technical Centre and Jordan Sims, a black militant at Eldon Avenue. Watson and others had succeeded in organising the Motor City Labor League together with white socialists, and they had launched a bookclub with 700, mostly white, members.

Unfortunately, ELRUM at least, refused to hand leaflets to white workers. Neither DRUM nor ELRUM encouraged white participation in their wildcats. Moreover, white sympathisers were told to form their own organisation. According to Mike Hamlin, '... we deliberately and consciously wrote off white workers'.[121]

With black workers suffering from the racism of foremen, most fellow workers and many union officials, black-only organisation was understandably attractive. But Watson and other leaders of the League were initially attracted to political activity in industry by the potential power of black workers to disrupt production. If that power was to be exercised it was necessary for black militants to lead black workers *and* white workers.

Black workers' organisations like DRUM are unstable. Either they must move towards black nationalist politics or towards uniting with white militants for the purpose of advancing class struggle. The logical extension of believing that the key to the black revolution is the black working class is an understanding of the need for working-class unity and the building of a revolutionary party. Black liberation can be achieved only as part of the struggle for socialism.

Chapter 5:
The Decline
of Black
Resistance

THE GARY Convention of March 1972 marked a turning-point for the US black movement. Its moving spirits included the cultural nationalist Amiri Baraka (LeRoi Jones), Charles Diggs, leader of the Congressional Black Caucus, and Jesse Jackson, the civil rights campaigner. The 3000 delegates agreed to a 'Black Agenda' which denounced 'white racism and white capitalism', and called for the formation of a new Black party. The nationalists were delighted that such a large and representative gathering had agreed to such a radical declaration. They were mistaken.

The convention did not *launch* a new party; it merely proposed it. The convention's real significance was that it demonstrated the wide-spread desire for the black movement to become an electoral move-ment. Many hoped that it would be a movement in opposition to the two big capitalist parties, but the more far-sighted recognised that since Blacks were only 11 per cent of the population, an independent black party could not succeed.

The shift away from movementist politics and towards institutional politics can be discerned in the careers of many of the activists. Ralph Abernathy, Martin Luther King's number two in the SCLC, became a supporter of Ronald Reagan. So too did Charles V Hamilton, co-author of the book **Black Power**. They joined a growing band of black Reagan supporters. However, the black Democrats were more significant. Seale and Newton joined up. Cockrel, once of DRUM, wanted to become mayor in Detroit. Andrew Young, another one-time leader of the SCLC, became Mayor of Atlanta, following his spell in the Carter administration. Jesse Jackson, yet another former lieutenant of Martin Luther King, won 26 per cent of the votes for the presidential nomination at the 1984 Democratic

Party Convention.

If Martin Luther King was the hero of the first period of post-war Black American politics, and Malcolm X the hero of the second, then today's hero is undoubtedly Jesse Jackson. Each symbolised an era and a mood. Malcolm X symbolised the demise of protest politics and the ascendancy of a revolutionary mood. Jesse Jackson symbolises the defeat of revolutionary nationalist politics and the ascendancy of middle-class blacks and electoral politics.

His particular talent was spotted by Martin Luther King. In the early 1960s he told Jackson: 'If you want to carve out your own niche in society, go ahead. But for God's sake don't bother me'. Soon after King's death Jackson broke with the SCLC and formed Operation PUSH.

PUSH made use of boycotts (or more commonly, the threat of boycotts) to persuade major companies to employ more Blacks, particularly as managers, to invest in black banks and to do business with black companies. Manning Marable argues that although PUSH achieved widespread publicity, it did little to reduce black unemployment. When thousands of black auto workers lost their jobs, Jackson's only response was to buy shares in the car companies in order to 'voice our concerns'. Jackson had an old message; 'Blacks need trade, not aid'. The aim was to assist individuals to advance within the system. The effect was 'to reinforce the capitalist spirit among those whom the system has most brutally exploited.'[1]

PUSH provided Jackson with a healthy income and a base for his political ambitions. Sometimes he would stay in the house of a poor Black in Harlem; most times he would stay in exclusive hotels. Furthermore, Jackson had the ability to make the prosaic act of voting sound like a crusade. 'There's a freedom train acomin',' he argued, 'but you've got to be a registered voter to ride'.

One of Jackson's most prominent supporters is Louis Farrakhan. He has a mass following among black Americans, partly because of his willingness to make anti-semitic statements. He has termed Judaism a 'dirty religion' and described Hitler as a 'great man'.[2] Farrakhan's message has an appeal to downtrodden poor Blacks. He is also supported by middle-class Blacks, and under his leadership the Nation of Islam has developed a network of small businesses. They are in no position to compete with big business but they, and the black middle classes generally, do compete with the

Jewish middle classes. Clearly there is no automatic unity among the oppressed!

Jackson has a broad base of electoral support, but his active backing comes from a much narrower section of the black population. This can be judged from the social composition of the black delegates at the 1984 Democratic Party Convention. Only 17 per cent had annual household incomes of less than $25,000; 41 per cent reported annual household incomes of $50,000 or more. In 1982, the median family income of black Americans was $13,598, and only 61,000 black families (or about 1 per cent) reported annual incomes exceeding $50,000.[3] Of the black delegates, 73 per cent had had a college education; in 1978 only 13 per cent of black Americans (from the same age band as most of the black delegates) had spent at least four years at college. Only 60 per cent of the white delegates to the Convention had a college education.

The groups recorded by the census as 'professional, technical, managerial or administration', increased from 7 per cent of the black population in 1960 to 17 per cent in 1980. The number of Blacks attending college increased from 75,000 in 1950 to 666,000 in 1976. By 1980 almost half of all black income was earned by one-fifth of all black families. There is a more specific group which has prospered in the period; black politicians. In 1964, only 103 blacks held elective office anywhere in the country. By 1983 the number of black officials exceeded 5,600, including 21 Congressmen and more than 200 mayors.[4]

It was this layer, the new black middle classes, who were the real victors of the revolutionary upsurge of the 1960s. The system could not concede an end to unemployment, poverty and unrewarding, unskilled labour. It could, however, provide a larger number of openings for black professionals and black politicians.[5]

However, for the mass of black Americans the situation has deteriorated. This can be seen most clearly from the unemployment statistics. In 1969, 6.7 per cent of blacks were unemployed; five years later the figure was 8.9 per cent; in 1979 it was 11.3 per cent; and in 1983 19.5 per cent. For black teenagers the unemployment rate in 1985 was about 50 per cent, and in some areas it reached 85 per cent. The ratio of black unemployment to white unemployment has also been increasing. In 1969 and 1973 the ratio was 2.1; in 1979 and 1983 it was 2.3. In part this is because of a decline in industries where a large number of Blacks have been employed, such as steel and cars. Meanwhile, black median family incomes have dropped to 53 per cent of the comparable white family incomes, the most significant gap in two decades.[6]

Black Democratic Party politicians have very different incomes, aspirations and life-styles from the mass of black Americans. Despite this, most black workers back these politicians, sometimes enthusiastically. The reasons for this are twofold. First, given the low level of class struggle, there is no real alternative for most workers. Republicans and white Democrats tend to appeal to higher income groups and tend to be more right-wing. Secondly, black candidates are sometimes forced to mount campaigns which become a real threat to corrupt and racist Democratic Party machines. This seems to have been the case in Chicago where Harold Washington's victory in 1983 over the Daly 'submachine' (which included his old police force chums) must have provided a rare pleasure for the thousands of Blacks and anti-establishment Whites who backed the campaign.[7]

However, the black politicians are likely to come into increasing conflict with their black (and white) working class electorate. Whether the politicians make their peace with the old party machines, or whether, by necessity or inclination, they build a new base in the bureaucracy, they will be forced to collaborate with big capital. Thus, after Andrew Young was elected in Atlanta he turned to the banks and corporations and said bluntly: 'I can win without you. I can't govern without you'. Johnny Ford, Mayor of Alabama and head of the National Conference of Black Mayors, has argued for a 'pro-business' outlook: 'We're about trying to get jobs. Dollars are the cutting edge.'[8]

Most dramatic, by far, was the police bombing of a section of Philadelpia in 1985, on the orders of its black Mayor, Wilson Goode. The bombing ignited a blaze which killed 11 Blacks and destroyed 62 black working-class homes. Its target was MOVE, a black counter-cultural group. It was claimed that automatic weapons and explosives were stored in the MOVE house, but none were found. Once in office Goode made use of the racist Philadelphia police in the same oppressive, unsympathetic manner as previous white mayors.[9]

The conflict of interests is likely to be increasingly marked in the case of public sector unions in cities with black mayors. For instance, in 1977 Atlanta's 900 black sanitation workers went on strike for higher pay. Three years earlier they had campaigned enthusiastically and successfully for the election of Maynard Jackson as the city's first black mayor. Jackson, who had failed to pay them any increase in wages, responded immediately: he sacked them all! The president of the sanitation workers' union, a white man with a history of support for civil rights causes, was condemned as a 'racist manipulator'. Jackson won the praise of big business, the media and leaders of the local black middle class.[10]

In the 1930s only 4 per cent of trade unionists were black. By 1970, however, there were more than 2.5 million black trade unionists in America, about 15 per cent of total union membership.[11] The recent recession and accompanying attack on trade unionism has brought an overall decline in membership, but there is no sign that black workers are becoming anti-union. Whatever the limitations of the unions, and no matter how few of the leading officials are black, if you are a black worker it is still better to be in the union than not. In 1970 non-white trade unionists received on average 83 per cent of the income of their white colleagues; Blacks outside the unions received only 62 per cent.[12]

Martin Luther King's words to the 1963 March on Washington, 'I have a dream', were a symbolic statement of 1960s optimism. For a small minority of America's black population the prospects are still promising. For the vast majority, optimism has turned to despair, and the 'dream' into a nightmare. For them the benefits of the 1960s proved few and transitory. Today racism exists with a vengeance. The system of which it is part turns life's daily toil into a daily misery. The electoral movement holds no answers for the majority of black Americans.

LESSONS FOR TODAY

We can list certain lessons that arise directly from the American experience.

Firstly, for the majority of black Americans separatism has not worked. The idea of a physical 'return' to Africa was a fantasy. Garvey's desire for the black man 'to have a country of his own', which would 'give him the opportunity to climb from the lowest to the highest position in a state of his own', on the other hand, has become a reality. Haile Selassie became emperor of Ethiopia. His dictatorship was bitterly resented by the majority of Ethiopians, and he was eventually removed in 1974.[13] Most of Africa is now independent, but the idea that the continent can provide a solution for black Americans is patently absurd. Terrible poverty is coupled, in most African countries, with very limited possibilities for political expression. Such problems are created by the international character of capitalism.

In practice separation came to mean a spiritual and/or economic separation within the United States. The most successful exponents of this approach were the Black Muslims under Elijah Muhammad. The Nation of Islam certainly made a few people very rich. It is likely that it also brought happiness to a larger number of black people by providing them with an existence cut off from many of the bitter realities of life in a racist society. But there can be no escape; and economic competition, unemployment and the police inevitably made their impact. Malcolm X recognised that the separatists were incapable of providing a solution for the majority of Blacks, and he rejected them to become more involved in the problems and politics of the wider society.

Secondly, the militant movements of the 1950s and 1960s won an end to legal segregation and the introduction of the right for every adult to be allowed to vote. They also helped to create an awareness within the ruling class, of the need for a larger layer of black people to have a material interest in the continuation of capitalism. Such 'concessions' were a blow to backward, mainly southern interests, but not to mainstream capitalism. On the contrary, they helped to stabilise the system. Today black people are still oppressed by racist police, racist bosses and racist workers. Unemployment among Blacks is now two to three times as high as in the mid-1960s. Integration into the system, in other words reformism, has not provided a solution to the problems of most black people.

Thirdly, the Panthers were well aware of the limitations of both segregation and integration, and chose a new, revolutionary road. Unfortunately, they based themselves on the *lumpen proletariat* rather than the proletariat proper. The former is an unstable and unreliable class, and because of its economic position is incapable of leading a revolution.

Fourthly, a revolution, by destroying the material basis of racism and inequality, could bring about black liberation, but in America such a revolution can only be achieved by black workers allying themselves with white workers. Blacks are too few in numbers to succeed alone. White workers are the only *other* group which has both the interest and the ability to fight for revolutionary change in society. Thus, black liberatioin can only be achieved by means of socialist revolution. For this it is necessary for socialists, black and white, to encourage united class struggle and to combat all divisions within the working class — in particular racism. This process is made more difficult if the best black militants are not organised alongside the best white anti-racists.

Finally, enormous objective problems inhibited the building of such an organisation. The overwhelming majority of white workers were thoroughly racist. The Panthers and the League, however, made two mistakes which led them to underestimate the potential for building a revolutionary organisation based on white as well as black workers.

They wanted to lead the masses in immediate revolutionary struggle. Their impatience led them to overestimate their own forces, and this led them into the ultra-leftism of armed actions and premature wildcat strikes. It also led them to underrate the *potential* for white workers to engage in mass struggles, and therefore the potential for the mass radicalisation of white workers. Just because white workers were not fighting did not mean they would never fight.

An objective, Marxist analysis of capitalism leads one to the view that competition forces the employing class to exact even greater concessions from the working class, and that these can be resisted only by means of struggle. Workers fight not because they want to, but because it becomes necessary. When white workers fight along-side black workers it becomes much easier to argue against their racial prejudices and argue for socialism. Some of the League's leaders understood this theoretically, but allowed themselves to be overinfluenced by their immediate experiences.

They underestimated the value of involving white workers and students in the building of a revolutionary organisation. The black struggles of the 1960s radicalised many whites, particularly students and young workers, and some of these were drawn towards the black revolutionaries. Many, riddled with liberalism and white guilt, would have been useless. Any that did not learn to work and socialise with black workers would have been discarded. Some, however, could have become valuable revolutionaries.

However no situation is static. The struggles of the 1950s, 1960s and early 1970s were the product of a particular conjuncture of forces. They produced a highpoint of black nationalist struggle which is unlikely to occur again. The black professional and managerial élite are becoming increasingly detached — economically, socially and politically — from working-class Blacks. This will not prevent sections of the middle classes form using nationalist rhetoric for opportunist purposes, but it is unlikely that the black middle classes will play the same radical role that they did in the 1960s. Working-class Blacks will have to look to themselves and their own struggles as a means to advance. When they do so they will have the possiblity of uniting with Hispanic and white workers, whose economic situation is little different from their own.

Our argument — that united class struggle provides the best means of advance for black workers — is likely to prove more valid with the passage of time. Revolutionary *nationalism* is the past. Revolutionary *socialism* is the future.

Lessons for Britain

The situation in Britain differs from that in the USA in many respects which strengthen our argument still further.

In the US 11 per cent of the population are black. In Britain Blacks are 3.5 per cent of the population. If revolutionary nationalists like the Panthers eventually failed in the US despite a high level of struggle, it is impossible to see how their kind of politics could succeed in Britain.

At the same time, Britain's black population is newer and has less tradition of uniting in struggle against white society. The possibilities of black unity are made more difficult by the different histories and cultures of Britain's black communities. West Indians and Asians have come to Britain at different times, often to work in different industries, and frequently to live in different parts of the country.

The racist police and media will naturally attempt to play up these differences between oppressed groups in order to increase the divisions between them. Socialists should avoid falling into this trap, since all black people suffer from racism. But it would be dishonest to pretend that differences do not exist, for they have a bearing on practice.

For instance, on 2 March 1981 there was a magnificent twelve-mile march from Deptford to Hyde Park in London called by the New Cross Massacre Action Committee. At least 10,000 people took part. The overwhelming majority were Afro-Caribbeans, with a small minority of Whites and a sprinkling of Asians. They chanted 'freedom' and 'justice'. Just over a month later, on 4 April, there was another major anti-racist demonstration, this time called by the Campaign against Racist Laws. About 20,000 people took part, chanting 'Black and White unite and fight' and 'Maggie out!' This time the great majority were Asians, mobilised particularly by the Sikh temples and the Indian Workers Associations, with a significant minority of Whites, and some West Indians.[14]

Racism in Britain also differs from that in America in important respects. Partly this is because for the British ruling class slave labour was never a major element in the domestic economy. The Jim Crow system and lynchings were never a feature of British life — although horrendous violence was meted out to Blacks overseas. British capitalism developed over a longer period and more slowly than American capitalism. It depended less upon immigrant labour and never cultivated the kind of ghettos which grew up around cities such as New York, Chicago and Detroit.

Inner-city Britain is quite different from ghetto America, where tens and sometimes hundreds of thousands of black people are concentrated in areas where virtually no white people live. Some inner-city areas in the US are now 90 per cent or even 100 per cent black. In Britain there are only three parliamentary constituencies (relatively small units, with fewer than 100,000 inhabitants) where the black population exceeds 40 per cent. This higher level of residential integration in Britain means that schools are more integrated and there is a greater chance of Blacks having white friends, and of Blacks marrying Whites.

Differences such as these lead to a different response to discrimination, inequality and racism. Take, for instance, the riots in British cities in 1981. Some commentators have described these as 'uprisings', and thereby equated them with the 1960s uprisings in America. There are some parallels. Antagonism to the police was a major factor in both cases, for example. But the analogy is in fact misleading.

First the British riots were on a much smaller scale. This can be seen from the number of participants — 1500 in Manchester was probably the largest; the number of deaths — only one, in Liverpool; and the amount of damage — in Brixton and Toxteth, probably the most violent, only a handful of buildings were actually destroyed. This is in complete contrast to the uprisings in Watts and Detroit.

Secondly, the American uprising were more political, in the sense that looting was more directed. In Watts, 'wherever a storekeeper identified himself as a "poor working negro trying to make business" or a "blood brother", the mob passed the store by.'[15]

Thirdly, and most significantly, the 'racial mix' of the participants was very different. The American uprisings were almost 100 per cent black. The exception was Detroit, where there were reports of a few white rioters and of 'some integrated gangs of looters'.[16] During the British riots, however, as Chris Harman writes:

>...the first Brixton riot broke when 'the police tried to arrest a black guy... black and white people went over to help'. 'The riot was... a fair cross-section of younger people, black and white...
>
>...in Bristol.. the crowd which drove back the police... was 'almost a third white' and 'if there was limited participation of Whites in the fighting, white people were heavily involved in the looting.' In the... first Southall riot... very few Whites were involved in the fighting. But the **Guardian** could write of the onlookers that 'one remarkable thing about the riot was the complete absence of racial tension among the white and Asian residents who mingled together...' ...A week later, '60 per cent of the rioters were Asian, the rest were West Indian and white.' In the case of Toxteth.. some white youths seem to have been involved from the beginning and by the end of the main night of rioting, the rioters were at least 50-50 black and white. In Moss Side, of the 106 arrests... 78 were white... In Wood Green... there were 'large numbers of Cypriot kids and West Indians and a slightly smaller number of Whites.' In Handsworth, the riots were 'black and white, but mostly Asian youths'. In Woolwich there were '250 Blacks and 50 Whites'... In Halifax there was 'a right good mix of skinheads and Asian youth'.

Harman contrasted the riots with American uprisings and concluded:

>There is one important — very important — difference, which if not taken account of completely distorts one's appreciation of the British events. In *virtually all* the British riots there has been significant white involvement alongside Blacks, and the involvement has not just been

of white leftists, but of white working-class youth.[17]

General attitudes on 'race' questions also differ markedly in Britain. In a recent survey only 38 per cent of British people interviewed said they thought racists should be allowed to hold meetings, compared with 56 per cent of Americans. The following table contrasts this with other opinions. In each case the figures give the percentage of people saying that the particular activity should be *allowed*:[18]

	USA	Britain
Protest meetings	74	85
Protest pamphlets	65	83
Protest marches and demonstrations	62	68
Revolutionaries — publish books	54	65
Revolutionaries — hold public meetings	53	52
Racists — publish books	55	51
Racists — hold public meetings	56	38
Revolutionaries — teach 15 year olds	19	12
Racists — teach 15 year olds	22	12
Organise nationwide strike	19	29
Publish government defence plans	15	24
Occupy government office	8	11
Damage government buildings	2	1

The difference on the 'race' questions is particularly marked. This perhaps reflects the point already made, that in Britain black and white working class people tend to be more integrated (with each other, not the system) than in America. However, in general, public opinions in Britain tend to be less reactionary than in America. Probably the main underlying reason for this is the greater strength of trade union organisation in Britain. The anti-collectivist, 'free-enterprise' ideology is more dominant in America than in Britain, reflecting a different reality. As we have argued earlier, this greater emphasis on competition in America would tend to create a more fertile climate within which racist ideas can prosper.

Whatever the validity of this analysis, there can be no doubt that trade union organisation is far stronger in Britain than in America. In 1985, 51 per cent of British employees were members of trade unions, compared to 18 per cent in America. In Britain as in America, a higher proportion of Blacks than Whites are members of trade unions. According to the PSI survey, 56 per cent of Asian and West Indian employees were union members, compared with 47 per cent of white employees. The survey concluded that, as in America, 'The greater propensity of black workers to join unions is largely a feature of the types of job they do.'[19] Of course a far higher proportion of Blacks in Britain are members of unions than is the case in America.

In a recent British survey 86 per cent of black people said that 'People of Asian/West Indian origin should join unions alongside white people', and only 4 per cent disagreed with this statement.[20] It is difficult to compare this with any American studies, but in 1966 only 43 per cent of black Americans said they thought that the unions had been 'helpful' to black people, while 13 per cent said they had been 'harmful'.[21]

The conclusion is clear: the prospects for black people to make progress by means of a nationalist or 'race first' strategy are even bleaker in Britain than in America. The prospects for advance by means of involvement in socialist politics and the class struggle are correspondingly greater.

BLACK NATIONALISM IN BRITAIN

In Britain as in America the revolutionary nationalism of the 1960s is in headlong retreat. The most prominent advocate of this current is the journal **Race Today**. In January 1986 this carried an editorial on the Tottenham riot which drew attention to the fact that the main spokesperson for the youths involved was Bernie Grant, who was 'close to fifty' and leader of the Labour-controlled local council. 'This is a very peculiar state of affairs,' **Race Today** commented. 'Young Blacks who led and participated in the revolt are in the main under 25, and not members of the Labour Party and hardly vote for it.'

'The continuing development of a radical and revolutionary culture is being undermined by the entry of educated young Blacks into the Labour Party,' said the article, lamenting: 'Where are the political journals, the newsletters, the pamphlets which circulated week after week in the black community only 18 years ago?'

The decline of black organisations outside the Labour Party has been associated with the increased involvement of Blacks in the party. This pattern is very similar to the shift which has occurred in America.

Two factors specific to the British context help to explain the drift of black activists into the Labour Party. In the first place, groups such as that around **Race Today** have placed great emphasis on the organisation and struggle of black workers, and have been hostile to the activities of middle-class elements within the black community. However, black workers have very rarely predominated in any strike. When they have, as at Grunwicks in North London in 1977, their situation has contradicted the black nationalist analysis.

The Grunwick strikers, mainly Asian women, and facing a vicious anti-union boss, won the active support of the best elements of a predominantly white labour movement. Socialists and militant trade unionists, including on one occasion Yorkshire miners and London dockers, most of them white, made up the bulk of the Grunwicks pickets. And it was the failure of the trade union leaders to support the strike which doomed it, like so many in which white workers were the overwhelming majority, to ultimate defeat.

In the absence of 'independent' action by black workers, the main form of struggle on which the black nationalists focussed were the riots of 1981 and 1985. But these were, as we have seen, to a large degree non-racial *class* riots in which white working-class youth participated alongside their black counterparts. Street movements of this kind are in any case volatile and temporary phenomena, exploding spontaneously and unpredictably into violent confrontations with the state, but dissolving just as suddenly into the apathy and isolation which preceded them. As the experience of the Panthers in the US showed, riots do not provide a stable basis for long-term organisation. The nationalists might act as cheerleaders, and often as self-appointed spokespeople for the youth on the streets, but the limelight would soon fade away, leaving them with as little real influence as before.

It should be no surprise that the most important arena of political activity for most black nationalists has been that of *defence* campaigns and related activities. Defence campaigns can be important, both for the individuals concerned and as a means of making propaganda against the state. However, even here the nationalists run into difficulties. For instance, following the 1981 riots there were some attempts to establish black-only defence campaigns in Brixton and elsewhere. This served to divide the defendants (many of whom were white) and confuse potential supporters, such as trade union organisations. It was of no assistance to the black defendants.

The inadequacies of black nationalism are not the only reason for its present weakness. Since the mid-1970s the working-class movement has itself been in retreat, faced with an increasingly confident and aggressive ruling-class offensive. Some of the most militant groups of workers have suffered terrible defeats — the miners above all. This has strengthened right-wing ideas within society generally, and within the labour movement. Especially after the miners' defeat, right-wing social democracy in the shape of Neil Kinnock and his supporters came to prevail within the Labour Party and the trade unions.

Black activists have been affected by this change in the balance of class forces. In the absence of a working class in the ascendant, they have had to choose between a feeble nationalist movement and the pursuit of reforms through the Labour Party. The latter seems more attractive, as well as more practical, offering the prospect of immediate gains — positive discrimination, police accountability, increased inner-city funding.

This willingness to seek reforms of the existing system involves an acceptance of the race relations 'industry'. The ruling class has since the 1960s pumped limited state funds into the black communities in the hope of buying off and integrating activists. This was, for example, the response of the Labour government to the Asian youth organisations which emerged in the mid-1970s. In the past, however, there was always a strong current of black militants who rejected these approaches. The growth of black reformism represents a much more widespread acceptance of the existing state. The black activists who have joined the Labour Party have not broken completely with nationalism — the rise of the Labour Party Black Sections is proof enough of this, but there has been a massive retreat from any frontal attempt to challenge the state.

In Britain as in America the black nationalists have been overtaken by black reformism. In both countries the growth of black reformism has been associated with the growth of a black middle class. In both countries this class, or a section of it, provides the main base of support for electoralist politics. In time of slump reformism cannot provide benefits for the majority, but it can provide assistance for individual members of the middle class. The parallel, however, should not be exaggerated. In Britain the black middle class is much weaker than in the US. In the class spectrum it is further from big business and nearer to the working class.

In Britain black reformism has developed along two parallel paths. Inside the Labour Party the Black Sections have provided the main focus; they will be considered in the next chapter. There has also been a growth of black members' groups inside some trade unions.

The more successful groups of black trade unionists have been set up in the white-collar sector, particularly among local government employees, members of NALGO. There have been few attempts to establish black workers' groups among manual workers, and those which have been set up have been unstable and shortlived.

For manual workers, promotion is a relatively unimportant means of advance. Collective action is far more important, both to defend wages and conditions and to prevent the excesses of racist supervisors. Black manual workers, therefore, must look to the union, and unity with white workers, to protect their interests. NALGO, by contrast, is a 'vertical' union, which organises not just poorly-paid clerical workers but also highly-paid managers and professional staff. For a large number of NALGO members promotion and individual advance are generally more important than collective action. The black members' groups may be a valuable means of applying pressure to obtain individual advance, but their exclusion of white workers means that they are incapable of successfully organising collective action. The black members' groups exist as a vehicle for an upwardly mobile section of black employees.

Black members' groups in NALGO were expanding during 1986 and into 1987. The defeats over the Tory government's 'rate-capping' of Labour-controlled councils had shown the union to be largely ineffective in defending its members' interests. As a result some of the black members, particularly in the higher grades, turned towards the black groups. Whereas DRUM in America ten years earlier was a product of struggle and conflict, the black members' groups in Britain in the 1980s were the product of retreat and compromise.

While socialists should defend the black members' groups against racist and right-wing attacks, it is important to point out that they contain certain dangers. This can be seen from the example at Camden in London, where one member of the black members' group is also the director of social services, a senior manager. At a group meeting in 1986 he argued against participation in the union, and as a result two black shop stewards resigned their union positions. In general the council appeared to be encouraging the black workers' group, at the expense of the union. It granted the group negotiating rights in certain areas and even made concessions which would not have been made to the union. The net effect, of course, was to weaken the union.

When it comes to any *major* issue — whether it is fighting for higher pay, opposing privatisation of services, or excluding a racist worker or manager — the ability to take collective action, and therefore unity with white workers, will be crucial. If the black workers' groups undermine union organisation they weaken the position of *all* workers, black and white.

In America and Britain the trends have been similar. Because the black nationalists were incapable of mounting a real challenge to capitalism their movement could not go forward. It collapsed into reformism. This happened because in Britain and America Blacks alone cannot overthrow the state. The best that is possible is a compromise — and compromise means the continuation of racism.

Chapter 6:
Labour and Racism

IN AMERICA the majority of Blacks have not benefitted from electoral politics. Could it be different in Britain? Is is possible that Black involvement with the Labour Party will transform its politics and its practice? Is it possible for the Labour Party to become a vehicle for advancing the interests of black people? Could it become effective in fighting racism?

Before we consider the Labour Party's Black Sections, it is worth recalling, briefly, Labour's record on racism. This will help us to understand the nature of the party which the Black Sections want to make use of in the fight against racism.

We have already seen how, during the 1960s and 1970s, the Labour Party capitulated to the racists on the issue of immigration. This was no exceptional event. Labour's history provides numerous examples of compromise with racism.

Among the most prominent of Labour's intellectuals in the party's formative years were Beatrice Webb and her husband Sidney (later Lord Passfield). Their views on 'race' were clearly influenced by their contemporaries, the social Darwinists.[1] 'Who could deny,' argued the Webbs, 'that the Pacific Islanders, the Malays, the Arabs, the Kaffirs, the Negroes, and all the indigenous inhabitants of the Asiatic mainland' were, in their 'capacity for corporate self-defence and self-government, *Non-adult races*'?[2]

The Webbs became particularly concerned about the decline in birth rates among Anglo-Saxon peoples. This could pose a major threat to the possibilities of introducing socialism, they said. It could mean that the one race which possessed those qualities most conducive to the development of socialism might be overrun by 'the offspring of the less thrifty, the less intellectual, the less farseeing races or classes'.[3]

Apparently these views were common in the Labour movement at the turn of the century.[4] Following the defeat of Russia in the war against Japan in 1905, an editorial in **Labour Leader** argued:

> Not Russia only, but Europe; and not only Europe, but the whole white race of the world has suffered a great defeat... we have pointed out that the war between Russia and Japan is a war between east and west, between the yellow race and the white race.[5]

Such views inevitably had some impact on the attitudes which Labour supporters adopted towards Jewish immigrants. For instance, in 1892, Robert Blatchford wrote a series of articles for his paper, the **Clarion**, under the title 'The invasion of England'. In them he queried the 'racial results likely to follow on the infusion of so much alien blood into the British stock'[6] Later, some articles in the **Clarion** presented an openly anti-Jewish position.

The Labour leadership eventually opposed the introduction of the 1905 Aliens Act. However, in the discussion about the Act, one of Labour's 'big four' leaders, J Bruce Glasier, indicated that the party was willing to relinquish its principles on the matter. His argument was just as opportunist as those of modern politicians:

> The belief that all men and nations are our brothers, even when they come to cut our throats or crowd us out of our workshops [can be taken too far]. I think we can better gain the confidence of the public, and thereby our position to exercise a useful influence by assuring the public that we understand and sympathise with the public feeling on this matter... We ought to make it clear that we recognise: that neither the principle of the brotherhood of man, nor the principle of socialist equality, implies that brother nations or brother man may crowd upon us in such numbers as to abuse our hospitality, overturn our institutions, violate our customs and oust us from our own jobs and homes, as has happened recently.[7]

In 1914, with war fever gripping the country and the House of Commons, the government put forward a new Aliens Registration Bill. This was passed within 24 hours, without a single vote against. A lone Labour voice raised in meek opposition was stifled by cries of 'sit-down'. Labour had been panicked into accepting stronger controls than those introduced in 1905, because, for the most part, they were willing to back a war against Germany.

In 1919, Labour opposed the introduction of a new Aliens Act.

What was acceptable in wartime was unacceptable in time of peace . Labour was then in opposition.[8] In 1924, however, they formed their first government. How would that affect their attitude towards anti-alien legislation?

In 1925 Major Yerburgh, a Tory MP, moved a motion that 'This House approves the possession by the House of full and sufficient authority to control alien immigration'. This rapidly exposed Labour's dilemma. John Scurr, 'an internationalist of the old socialist school',[9] who was himself opposed to immigration control, moved a compromise amendment which opposed the present rules, but accepted the need for immigration control.

> Scurr, goaded by Tory interruptions, could not restrain his basic principles ... 'We are not afraid to say that we are internationalists — all of us (laughter). The boundaries between nations are artificial.'
>
> The Labour leaders writhed on their benches. They understood what the more naive Scurr did not: that immigration control is imposed in the interests of the people of one nation — not all nations. Macdonald, Thomas, Clynes and the rest had already rejected internationalism in their struggle for parliamentary power.[10]

John Clynes was labour's first Home Secretary. He must have gladdened the heart of many a Tory. It was a good thing, he argued, that people should have to pay a £10 naturalisation fee, even though this was more than most working-class people could possibly afford. He then bragged that he had naturalised fewer Russians than his Tory predecessor.[11] Clynes used the Act in 1929 to refuse asylum to Leon Trotsky. Paul Foot comments:

> The 'right of asylum', if it ever existed, had been buried by a Labour government. It is ironical that Karl Marx, Frederick Engels and Lenin had all lived in Britain under Tory and Liberal governments. Yet the fourth of that revolutionary quartet was banned by a Labour government.[12]

Labour's identification with the 'national interest' undermined its commitment, which was never strong, to the free movement of labour. Socialist sympathy for fellow workers from other lands was replaced by nationalist antipathy to 'aliens' and 'immigrants'. In acceding to anti-alien legislation Labour had accepted that Britain and the British must come first, a proposition that was overtly nationalist and unconsciously racist.

Imperialism

Defence of the 'national interest' also justified defence of British imperialism, and we have already seen how imperialism has been a major material force sustaining racism. Labour's leaders have concurred with almost every significant imperialist engagement, and every time this has given a further boost to racism. Labour leaders might deny their acquiescence, but the record speaks against them. For instance James Byrnes, the American Secretary of State, just after the Second World War said of Labour government policy at that time:

> Britain's stand was not altered in the slightest, so far as we could discern, by the replacement of Mr Churchill and Mr Eden by Mr Attlee and Mr Bevin. This continuity of British foreign policy impressed me.[13]

In 1939 Attlee had argued: 'We should make it clear by deed as well as by words that we are standing for democracy and not for imperialism.'[14] George Orwell commented that this kind of claim rested upon 'an unspoken clause ... "not counting niggers".'[15] On the question of India, throughout the war Attlee supported Churchill, who had described Gandhi as 'a naked little fakir'. He even went as far as supporting the 'Whipping Act' and internment without trial. At the time the Labour Party national executive resolved:

> The Labour Movement is compelled to regard the present attempt to organise civil disobedience in India as certain to injure seriously the hope of Indian freedom... the Labour Movement therefore considers that the action of the government of India in detaining the leaders of Congress was a timely and unavoidable precaution.[16]

After the war Attlee, now prime minister, sent gunboats to intimidate the democratically elected government of Iran when it threatened to nationalise the Anglo-Iranian oil company. The Labour government suppressed workers who in the late 1940s and early 1950s were in the forefront of the independence movements in Ghana, Nigeria and Kenya. In Nigeria, the police shot dead 18 striking miners at Enugu.[17] In Kenya, they precipitated a general strike by barring the East African TUC and arresting its leaders; then broke the strike using low-flying planes, armoured cars and mass arrests.[18] The Attlee government supported a massive military campaign in Malaya in an attempt to crush the Communists. These are but a few examples to indicate that the most 'left-wing' of Labour governments was pro-imperialist. Their general concern was to create governments which would be sympathetic to British interests. Democracy, let along internationalism, was not their concern.

Racism was always implicit in these actions. Sometimes, however, it was explicit in the attitudes of Labour ministers. Hugh Dalton, a cabinet minister from 1940 to 1947, provides us with one example. When he was offered the Colonial Office by Attlee in 1950, he was horrified and commented: 'I had this horrid vision of pullulating, poverty stricken, diseased nigger communities, for whom one could do nothing in the short run and who, the more one tries to help them, are querulous and ungrateful'.[19]

Another example is provided by Patrick Gordon Walker, who was Commonwealth Secretary in 1950, and in that capacity banned the Botswanan leader, Seretse Khama, from returning to his own country because he had married a white woman. Walker defended his position as follows:

> The right of mixed marriages has never been challenged, and never will be. But what *we had to decide* was whether a particular mixed marriage of a man who was to rule a country was in the interests of that country.[20]

In the post-colonial era there has been a decline in this kind of paternalism. However, subsequent Labour leaderships have failed to face up to and reject this contemptible record. From time to time, paternalistic attitudes still show through. Recently, Labour leader Neil Kinnock defended Roy Hattersley's use of the phrase 'my Asians' to describe Asian members of the Sparkbrook constituency. Hattersley was, however, quite rightly condemned by Sharon Atkin, of the Labour Party's Black Sections, for his 'patronising and condescending attitude.'[21]

From the First World War, through Harold Wilson's support for the Americans in Vietnam, support for British rule in Northern Ireland, to the 1982 Falklands War, Labour's leaders have sided with imperialism. In the case of the Falklands War, Neil Kinnock argued in favour of sending the British Naval Task Force, saying it was 'necessary and unavoidable'. Labour's leader at the time was Michael Foot. He attempted to prove he was a better imperialist than Margaret Thatcher by arguing in the House of Commons:

> So far, the Falkland Islanders have been betrayed. The responsibility for the betrayal rests with the government. The government must

prove by its deeds — they will never be able to do it by words — tha
they are not responsible for the betrayal and cannot be faced with that
charge![22]

Labour leaders rarely express their support for imperialism in openly racist terms. However, the fact that they are supporters of imperialism means that they cannot undermine the racism which it inevitably encourages. That racism is based on an underlying, but rarely expressed view, that the British are in some way superior to the Germans, Indians, Africans, Irish or Argentinians.

The state

Labour's belief in a 'national interest' is crystallised in their understanding of the state. They view it as neutral in class terms. They believe that it can play a progressive role in carrying through social and economic reforms. All that is necessary is for parliament to pass the correct legislation. Whatever one's views about a particular official or a certain piece of legislation, the state and the laws should be honoured and obeyed. This view has important implications for racism. It has led Labour to support the institutions of the state, no matter how racist these are in practice.

The function of immigration officers is to implement immigration legislation, the very basis of which is discrimination against black people. Hardly surprising, then, that the immigration service should be riddled with racism. In 1955, when the Tory cabinet considered introducing immigration controls but had qualms about appearing racist, the Home Secretary, Gwilym Lloyd George, made an interesting suggestion. If the right to refuse admission were given to the immigration officers, he argued, they would see that only black people were kept out![23]

A few years ago the majority of immigration officers left their union, the Society of Civil and Public Servants (SCPS), to form a racist breakaway organisation, the Immigration Service Union. It was the action of these officers which provoked the Tory government's decision in 1986 to introduce new visa requirements for visitors from certain black Commonwealth countries. Labour criticised the Tory proposals as racist — which they were — but the only alternative they could offer was to propose the recruitment of more immigration officers; that is, more recruits for a notoriously racist arm of the state.

...so clear evidence that racism has become ...d in the courts, the probation services and prisons,[24] ...lem is greatest in the police force. In an extensive survey ...ut by the Policy Studies Institute in 1982, nearly two-thirds ...est Indians questioned said that they were treated worse by the ...lice than were white people. Only one per cent considered they were better treated. When it came to discrimination the police were thought to be far worse than pubs, schools or even the courts.[25] Consequently few Blacks are recruited to the police force. By 1981, after much effort, the London Metropolitan Police had boosted the number of black officers in the force to 132, or half of one per cent of the total.[26]

There is a simple reason for this state of affairs. The police are thoroughly racist. It hardly seems necessary to demonstrate this point. Even the Home Office's own researchers have accepted that the police continue to stereotype black people and treat them with greater suspicion and hostility.[27] A PSI study conducted on behalf of the Metropolitan Police provided ample evidence of a racist police culture where terms such as 'wog', 'coon', 'spade', and 'monkey' seem to have become the norm.[28]

This is the background to the Tottenham riot of 1985. Bernie Grant, the black leader of labour-controlled Haringey Council, commented after the riot:

> I condemn the police action and do blame them for the death of Mrs Jarrett... The youths reacted to years of oppression by police... The police... got... a bloody good hiding.[29]

Grant was reflecting a widespread mood among black people in Haringey, but his comments proved an embarrassment to the Labour Party leadership. Goaded by the press, first Roy Hattersley and then Neil Kinnock dissociated themselves from his remarks. Two days later a thousand white council workers joined a racist march protesting against Grant. The gutter press were loving it, and plumbed new depths with headlines such as 'Barmy Bernie moves in with blonde' and 'Black Bernie quitting wife for white girl'.[30] Not once did Kinnock criticise the racism of the police or the media. His strictures were reserved for the youths involved in the riot and for Bernie Grant, a member of his own party. A combination of electoral considerations and a desire not to undermine the police had helped to fuel a racist backlash.

There are substantial reasons why — even with the best of intentions — Labour cannot stamp out racism in the police force. First there is the impact of the immigration laws, which define black people as the problem. If the police are to catch 'illegal immigrants', discover alleged 'fake' marriages, track down overstayers and enforce deportation orders they have to look, in the main, for blacks.[31] The anti-immigrant laws have lent legal respectability to ages old and widely accepted racial prejudice.

Secondly, racism is, in practice, encouraged by senior officers. For instance, following the Brixton riot of 1981 and some rather mild criticism by Lord Scarman, the Metropolotan Police decided to justify their actions by raising, once again, the bogey of 'mugging'. They produced figures which purported to show that black people were particularly prone to involvement in this form of crime. There were a number of disturbing features about this incident.[32] Most significantly, 'mugging' was the only 'crime' for which the police gave a racial breakdown. They justified their statement in terms of public interest. The evidence for public interest? A number of articles in the press. The source of these articles? The police![33]

Because the police believe that Blacks and particularly West Indian youth, are more likely to be engaged in criminal activity than Whites they stop them for questioning much more often.[34] This has two important effects. The correlation between Blacks and crime becomes a self-fulfilling prophecy, thus justifying the initial prejudice of the police. But it fuels the general resentment felt by black people, and black youth in particular. On occasion this will manifest itself in demonstrations and riots. Blacks then become a public order problem: opponents of the *status quo*. However, unlike other public order problems — 'reds', pickets, peace campaigners and the like — they are constantly visible and constantly subject to police harassment. Racism has become part of the structure of the police's relationships with black people.

There is a third factor. As argued elsewhere, in other jobs there is the possibility that racists may be isolated by the unity that comes from the experience of class struggle. This — the key to undermining racism — is not an option open in the police. On the contrary, any initial prejudice is constantly reinforced by fellow members of this tightly knit community. Furthermore, the nature of police work and the history of police action tends to attract recruits with conservative and authoritarian personalities.[35] In 1982, a lecturer at Hendon Police College produced essays which demonstrated that Metropolitan Police trainees were overwhelmingly and strongly prejudiced against Blacks. The lecturer, John Fernandez, was promptly sacked.[36]

As the crisis of capitalism deepens, and as resentment and resistance increase, the prime function of the police becomes clearer. For the ruling class, they are the first line of physical defence in the class war. The police attacks on pickets at Grunwicks, Warrington, Orgreave and Wapping have shown this clearly. To maintain the allegiance of individual officers in such circumstances a set of ideas which both explains their experiences and binds them to the ruling class is necessary. Authoritarianism and racism fit the bill well.

Racism in the police force is not a reflection of racism in society, it is a reflection of the role that the police play within society. That role is politiely described as 'maintaining order'. In reality this means suppressing discontent from below. Such suppression is a reactionary business which requires reactionary ideas. So long as Neil Kinnock supports this business, he will be forced to tolerate the reactionary ideas. He may abhor racism in the police force, he may even legislate against it, but he will not be able to eradicate it or even significantly reduce it. Racism underpinned the 1985 killing of Cynthia Jarret in Haringey and the disturbance which followed. What was Kinnock's response? Support for the police. What was the effect? Racism was reinforced.

This brief survey of Labour's rotten record establishes one point. Labour's politics are based on compromise. It is their desire that capitalism and the capitalist state should act in the interests of the majority; but they lack the power to make this possible. Consequently, they compromise. Limited changes are proposed, because they lack the forces to bring about change which is fundamental.

Labour's ideology is based upon this process of compromise. 'National interest' attempts to unify the contradictory interests of workers and capitalists. The Webbs' 'racist socialism' reflected a compromise between two sets of ideas representing two antagonistic class forces. They lacked a systematic attachment to the working class, and allowed themselves, therefore, to be influenced by those bourgeois ideas which were predominant at the time.

Labour politicians are no doubt genuine in their desire to rid the police and the immigration service of racism. The problem is, however, that racism is endemic within the police, and immigration controls are inherently racist. Since Labour lacks the ability to dispense with either the police or the controls, it is forced to propose utopian solutions for both: non-racist police, non-racist immigration controls. These are compromise formulas.

Racism is a product of capitalist society. Labour dislikes both, but because it cannot eradicate capitalism, it is forced to tolerate racism. It compromises. And every time it compromises it encourages the continued existence of racism. Labour is not consistently racist, but it cannot be consistently anti-racist.

LABOUR'S BLACK SECTIONS

Black Sections supporters accept that Labour has a racist past. However, they believe that by organising within the party they can transform it into a vehicle for black people's interests. The result, they believe, will be the adoption by a future Labour government of policies which undermine racism and advance black people — for example through the use of positive discrimination in favour of Blacks and other oppressed groups. To some degree Black Sections have had an opportunity to implement such policies locally, through their involvement in left-wing Labour-controlled councils.

At a national level, the Black Sections strategy bears a strong resemblance to that pursued by Tony Benn and the Labour left in the late 1970s and the early 1980s: first change the party, then use it as a means of winning reforms through the state apparatus. The Black Sections, however, have had even less success than the Labour left. At the 1986 party conference the Black Sections won only one vote out of five. The bulk of the trade union block vote was firmly wielded to back up Neil Kinnock's unremitting hostility towards them.

Kinnock opposes the Black Sections' call for separate black organisation inside the Labour Party by saying this would amount to the introduction of 'segregation'.[37] But since other groups — women, youth, Zionists — are granted representative rights within the party, why should Blacks be denied the same status? Roy Hattersley went even further, and compared supporting the Black Sections to backing apartheid.'[38] This turns reality on its head. Apartheid is the creation of a powerful and privileged minority seeking to maintain its dominance. Black Sections are a response by an *oppressed* group to the racism, not just of British society generally, but of the Labour Party itself. The Labour leadership's response is to equate the demands of the oppressed with the policies of their oppressor. Kinnock's and Hattersley's pious 'anti-racism' is merely a veneer concealing acceptance of the racist *status quo*.

Just as socialists have a duty to support the right of black people to organise against their oppression and to defend themselves, so they must support the demands of the Black Sections for official recognition and separate representation within the Labour Party. But equally we have the right to question whether the Black Sections' strategy will advance the interests of black people.

The fundamental issue is whether the Black Sections can change the Labour Party. Kinnock's opposition to them did not mean that he personally was a racist. Rather it flowed from the nature of Labourism itself. Labour is an electoral party, which seeks to achieve change by winning a majority of seats in parliament. The party is about winning elections, and this shapes the way it operates. Above all, in conditions when the working class is in retreat, it makes left-wing politics a liability, especially at election times. Working people participate in elections as passive, isolated individuals subject to a huge barrage of right-wing propaganda from the mass media. Fighting on this terrain, Labour leaders and activists are under enormous pressure to steer rightwards, towards the 'middle ground'.

Kinnock's strategy after Labour's catastrophic defeat in the 1983 election was to turn the party into what left-wing MP Eric Heffer aptly called an 'SDP Mark II'. This involved breaking the power of the left on the national executive and witch-hunting the Militant Tendency.

In the wake of the miners' defeat, and with another election looming, the Tories began to concentrate their fire on 'loony left' Labour councils, many of which were led by Black Sections supporters — Bernie Grant in Haringey, Linda Bellos in Lambeth, Merle Amory in Brent. In these circumstances Kinnock's opposition to the Black Sections reflected his fear that they would prove as big an electoral liability as Militant or Arthur Scargill.

In this he had the support of the trade union bureaucracy, whose votes control party conferences. The union leaders are a profoundly conservative force within the labour movement, wedded to the pursuit of compromise with capital. Their interests lie in the election of a Labour government to preside over and encourage negotiations between unions and employers. Consequently the role of the trade union bureaucracy is to buttress Labour's electoralism, and to support the leadership in its efforts to rid the party of embarrassing left-wing associations.

The defeat of the Black Sections at successive party conferences was therefore no accident, but reflected the conflict between the aspirations of black activists and the requirements imposed by Labour's basic drive to win elections. Moreover, while the Black Sections have been in opposition to the party leadership nationally, many of their most prominent members hold office locally in Labour-controlled inner-city councils. They have proved no better at running the 'local state' to the benefit of working-class people than past Labour governments.

Councils with black leaders, like other left-led councils, proved ineffective in opposing Tory rate-capping legislation designed to cut local spending and services. Faced with the threat of disqualification, left-wing councillors who had pledged themselves to defy the law, with the backing of the 1984 party conference, soon capitulated. The one council to hold out, Liverpool, was left to fight on alone and its leaders expelled from the Labour Party.

This surrender in the face of state power meant that the left-wing councils had to implement increasingly savage cuts on the Tories' behalf. As these cuts frequently resulted in redundancies, they inevitably meant clashes between the councils and their own employees. In this climate, the way in which left-wing councils set out to implement anti-racist policies sometimes made things worse. In part, of course, this reflected the influence of racist ideas among council workers, but at the same time they could see councils placing ever greater emphasis on the struggle against racism while doing nothing to defend the jobs and living standards of the workers they represented and employed.

Moreover, there was a tendency to impose anti-racist policies *from above*, rather than arguing for them politically among the council workforce. This approach — bureaucratic anti-racism — is well captured by an interview with a NUPE shop steward working for Camden council:

'The council is quite right to bring in an equal opportunities policy and to take on racism,' said Alan Walter... Councillors, with the support of shop stewards, could and should have addressed meetings of the workforce to explain their policy and at the same time the problems the borough faces through ratecapping.

Instead, they used supervisors and foremen to 'motivate' the council's policy among the workers they control. Nothing could have been worse. It was an invitation for people to make racist jokes as a gesture against their managers. Worse, some supervisors made the whole issue into a farce. Many are themselves racist and use racism to help keep control of the workforce.

'The result was appalling,' said Alan.[39]

Instead of seeing the council workers and their unions as potential allies in the fight against racism, they were seen as enemies on whom anti-racist policies had to be imposed. The councils aimed to reduce racism, but the way in which their policies were implemented meant that sometimes they had the reverse effect: rather than the hard-line racists being isolated, their support was increased.

An example of this is the way Haringey council handled Brian Berrett, the racist who led the demonstration of the council's workers against council leader Bernie Grant after the Tottenham riot. The council could have sacked Berrett for contravening its anti-racist policy; instead he was removed for technical breach of a loan agreement he had with the council. His fellow workers, including some black employees, saw this as a case of victimisation — and went out on strike. Had the council campaigned alongside anti-racist workers on the basis that Berrett was a racist and therefore a threat to trade union unity, they might have isolated him. Instead they appeared as opponents of trade unionism and turned Berrett into a hero.

Another example of the disastrous consequences of bureaucratic anti-racism is provided by the McGoldrick affair in Brent in 1986. The leader of Brent council at the time was Merle Amory, a supporter of the Black Sections, and the council's principal race relations adviser was Russell Profitt, a Black Section member and Labour's prospective parliamentary candidate.

In their enthusiasm to use their powers against a 'racist', the council suspended Maureen McGoldrick, a primary school head teacher, for an alleged racist remark. This she denied, and the council was never able to sustain its case. She was backed by the National Union of Teachers and by parents at her school, many of them black. Eventually, after strikes and threats of further strikes, High Court actions and threats of further actions, the council backed down.

In the course of pursuing their campaign against Maureen McGoldrick, the council severely damaged the credibility of their own anti-racist policies. They saw themselves as stick-wielding employers handing down punishment from on high. Inevitably many of their employees came to see them in the same light.

These two cases have in comon a failure to distinguish between, on the one hand, white workers influenced by racist ideas, and on the other, *organised racists*. The majority of white workers in Britain are in all likelihood influenced to some degree by racist ideas. This does not mean they cannot be won away from these idea, given struggles which widen their horizons and consistent opposition to racism by socialist fellow workers. But there is also a tiny minority of organised racists, some of them members or sympathisers of Nazi groups, who actively spread racist ideas in their workplaces and harass black people. Any strategy for fighting racism which is to be effective must aim to isolate this minority.

Too often, however, left-wing councils have ignored this distinction. Council employees who may have accommodated to racist ideas have been treated as if they were fascists who deserved the sack, while some councils have gone to the opposite extreme. In 1985 Islington council refused to sack a group of organised racists among their employees, even breaking a strike of other workers demanding the group's dismissal.

These episodes are not isolated mistakes. They are evidence of a mistaken approach. Just as Labour governments identify with and defend the British state, so Labour-controlled councils, even those led by members of the Black Sections, identify with the power of their office. Because change is seen as coming from above, organised groups of workers are seen as an obstacle. This inevitably encourages resentment and resistance, which will sometimes take on a racist or reactionary character.

In the final analysis, the politics of the Black Sections is not qualitatively different from that of the Labour leadership. They too accept the priority of winning votes. They too wish to use the existing state rather than develop struggles against it. The Black Sections have not in general engaged in mass campaigns. Their energies have been directed towards gaining influence inside the party, winning elections and running councils, rather than building mass support for campaigns against deportations and racist violence. Getting elected comes first. Black Sections activists are consequently subject to all the temptations of careerism, just like other Labour politicians. Those most likely to be elected to parliament have all, at one time or another, shown that they are willing to compromise principles in the pursuit of electoral appeal.

In Tottenham, Bernie Grant had to endure a vile and racist media campaign coupled with public criticism by the Labour leadership. He did not survive without compromising his own principles. Initially he said of the rioters: 'I will not condemn them or their actions.'[40] Four days later, following pressure from Neil Kinnock, he agreed to a council resolution condemning the rioters,[41] while at the same time the council quietly dropped its plan to block the borough's contribution to Metropolitan Police funds.[42]

To give another example, in the safe Labour parliamentary seat of Hackney North, Diane Abbott from the Black Sections defeated Ernie Roberts to secure the Labour Party nomination. Ernie Roberts was one of the few solid and reliable 'hard left' members of parliament, a founding member of the Anti Nazi League and himself a supporter of the Black Sections with a proven record of defending black and trade union struggles. Diane Abbott commented : '... it's obvious that the people of Hackney were fed up with having a 73-year-old white man as their MP.'[43] As far as she was concerned, it seems, physical attributes are more important than politics.

The leading lights of the Black Sections have come from an upwardly mobile layer of 'caring' professionals: lawyers, senior local government administrators and trade union officials. They lacked the base among class-conscious black workers which might impose some degree of accountability. Nor did they seek to develop such a base. As their careers develop they will be tempted to identify, as have so many other Labour politicians before them, with 'the interests of the community as a whole' and 'the national interest' — neither of which offers any answer to the problems faced by black people in Britain.

RACISM AND REFORMISM

Because the Labour Party attempts to reconcile contradictory class interests, it is itself a contradictory phenomenon. The differences between the Black Sections on the one hand and Neil Kinnock on the other reflect this. As Tony Cliff and Donny Gluckstein put it: 'the Labour Party... expresses both the workers' opposition to the social *status quo* and at the same time blunts that opposition.'[44] We might add that it expresses an opposition to racism, but blunts that opposition. It attempts to channel the aspirations of black people, particularly black workers; but at the same time it has to secure the support of racist voters and a racist state machine. So it compromises; it attempts to blunt those aspirations.

This process leads to a compromising of principle and to inconsistency. This can be seen in the welcome given by Ben Tillet, who later became a Labour MP, to the newly-arrived Jewish workers: 'Yes, you are our brothers and we will do our duty by you. But we wish you had not come.'[45]

The Labour Party justifies its compromises by reference to interests which are supposed to be higher, more important, than those of class: national interests and community interests. In the process attempts are made to separate ideas from the material forces which sustain them. The division between bourgeois ideology — racism for instance — and proletarian ideology — which counterposes internationalism to racism — is fudged, and socialism is redefined. For instance Ramsey MacDonald, Labour's first prime minister, argued that:

> Socialism marks the growth of society, not the uprising of a class. The consciousness which it seeks to quicken is not one of economic class solidarity, but one of social unity and growth towards organic wholeness ... Socialism is no class movement... It is not the rule of the working class: it is the organisation of the community.[46]

This separation of ideas from their material base, otherwise known as idealism, is common among reformist intellectuals and has an impact on their approach to racism. In particular, attempts are made to disconnect racism from capitalism. This is clearly the view of Neil Kinnock, who in 1986 told the **New Statesman** that racism was not related to 'history' or 'property values', but concerned 'ridiculous superstitions about the nature of black skin.'[47]

This separation of racist ideas from their material roots justifies Labour's rejection of the view that class struggle is a means of overcoming racism. If racism is a matter of wrong ideas, superstitition, then it needs only to be challenged with the right ideas; the racists, 'Whites first' ideology can be countered with the assertion 'One race, the human race'.

If this is the ground on which racism is to be challenged, of course, there is no reason why Labour should not team up with the Tories, the brickie with the bishop, the worker with the employer. In practice, however, this approach is likely to be ineffective, as the following example shows.

In 1968 London dockers were threatened, not only by rising inflation and a wage freeze — which they shared with the rest of Britain's workers, but in particular by the containerisation of international trade and the mechanisation of dockwork. As work could be seen leaving the docks, 'immigrants' could be seen arriving from Tilbury. Enoch Powell's 'rivers of blood' speech made an impact on the dockers precisely because it focussed on existing anxiety. It struck a chord when he argued that 'the sense of alarm, and of resentment, lies not with the immigrant population but with those among whom they have come and are coming.'[48] The immigrant threat was, of course, an illusion, but the 'sense of alarm and resentment' was real.

Powell received strong support in the docks. Militants there were thrown into confusion. Some were swayed by the racists. Some hid. The only practical suggestion was that a priest should be invited to address the dockers on the evils of racism. This is the kind of solution which flows from Labour-type politics,[49] opposing racism on moral grounds without relating to the real reasons for the 'alarm and resentment' — the employers' increasing attack on jobs. The moral approach proved worse than useless; the dockers marched out on strike in support of Powell.

The separation of racism from its material base provides justification for Racism Awareness Training, which has become popular with local authorities (many of them led by Black Section and Labour left supporters). It is also used by some large corporations. It operates on the assumption that Whites are inherently racist, and that the key to undermining racism is for Whites to be made aware of their own prejudice. If a few individuals adopt more enlightened views as a result of this training, it has no effect on the material factors which are constantly stimulating racism. As one socialist put it:

> Racism Awareness Training doesn't operate on class lines, but on individual feelings and experiences. How otherwise could health authorities hold racism awareness training courses for senior managers, then, confident that they have confronted their own racism, implement privatisation policies which mean redundancies for large numbers of black workers?[50]

While it would be wrong for socialists to oppose awareness training, there is a danger that it will redefine anti-racism as a series of 'guilt trips'. A well organised collection in support of black workers on strike in South Africa would be far more effective in countering racism. 'Racism Awareness Training' provides an alibi for those who want to oppose racism without getting their hands dirty; it is about anti-racism without class struggle.

The idealist view of racism leads to moralism: the view that one should oppose racism because it is 'bad'. This argument has little appeal to the white worker who believes he cannot get a housing transfer because the 'Pakis' are getting all the houses. An argument about how Tory government policies are forcing the sale of council houses and preventing the building of new ones might be more successful.

There are many people in the Labour Party, and particularly in the Black Sections, who recognise that racism is not just a matter of ideas; they recognise institutional racism as well. But they then proceed to separate the two, trying to solve the first by moral arguments and the second by imposing administrative changes.

Material conditions, however, have a way of re-asserting themselves. There is massive inequality between Blacks and Whites in jobs and housing. Policies that aim to increase the proportion of Blacks in work and with decent homes are therefore clearly correct. But at a time of Tory-imposed cuts in Council housing and jobs, when there are fewer resources to go round anyway, 'positive discrimination' in favour of black people runs the risk of provoking a racist backlash.

Eamonn McCann has argued that one reason for the Loyalist backlash in Northern Ireland in 1968 was the attempt by the government to introduce policies reducing the discrimination against Catholics in jobs and housing without increasing the total number of jobs and houses. Many poor Protestant workers believed that the policies would be implemented at their expense.[51]

A successful fight against racism must be linked to material advance, and that material advance requires the strengthening of trade union organisation. Successful class struggles have two effects where racism is concerned. Firstly they ensure more resources for the working class — whether as a result of pay increases or through forcing government and local authority policies that benefit the class as a whole. This makes it possible to improve the position of black workers without Whites feeling threatened. Secondly they encourage *class* unity, in other words the unity of black and white, and so undermine racism.

But the Labour Party, once in office, claims decisions concerning the nature and pace of change as its prerogative. When workers take industrial action in an attempt to bring about even a small shift in the balance of wealth and power this is seen as 'unwarranted interference'. The party leadership sees the working class, or at least its organised sections, as an obstacle. Strikes and threats of strikes are met with opposition. Where possible deals are struck with trade union leaders: tea and biscuits at Number Ten. When necessary, Labour will use the force available through the state: whether through legislation, such as Harold Wilson's imposition of statutory wage controls, or directly such as the use of the army to break the 1977 firemen's strike.

Either way, the effect is to discourage workers from uniting in struggle. The opportunities for black and white workers to discover their common interests are thereby reduced. If the holding back of workers' struggle leads to a decline in living standards, which it frequently does, then fertile conditions are created for the seeds of racism to sprout and grow.

Racism has reached a high pitch twice since 1945 — and both times the Labour Party was in office. The first time was in 1968, when London dockers and meat-porters marched in support of Enoch Powell. The second was between 1976 and 1979, with the street marches and electoral successes of the Nazi National Front. Both movements reflected the demoralisation of workers who had elected a Labour government only to find it enacting policies which were against the interests of workers. Both also reflected the confusion this fostered among trade unionists.

A conflict between Labour's principles and its practice lies at the heart of reformism. They may want to construct socialism, but they deny themselves the tools to do so. In principle they favour working people, but in practice they undermine us. In rejecting class struggle as a means of establishing socialism, Labour blunts the fight against racism. In rejecting the arguments of class struggle as a means of countering racist ideas, Labour disarms anti-racists.

Chapter 7:
The Revolutionary Socialist Alternative

REVOLUTIONARY SOCIALISM differs fundamentally from both black nationalism and reformism. It treats the working class as the subject not the object of change. It believes that white workers have a material interest in combatting racism. It predicts that black and white workers can be forged into a revolutionary class in the course of mass struggles. How can these ambitious claims be defended?

The theory of class struggle on which revolutionary socialism is based was outlined by Karl Marx in the middle of the last century. Marx's contribution was, in his own words:

> (1) to show that the *existence of classes* is simply bound up with *certain historical phases of the development of production;* (2) that the class struggle necessarily leads to the *dictatorship of the proletariat;* (3) that this dictatorship itself only constitutes the transition to the *abolition of all classes* and to a *classless society.* [1]

This transition from capitalist society to a workers' state, and later to communism, is important for our analysis of racism.

We have seen how the principal material basis for racism is the competition central to capitalism, which encourages competition within the working class for jobs, houses and even marriage partners. This creates divisions within the working class and helps deflect attention from the real causes of poverty and inequality. Racial or ethnic divisions are especially valuable to the ruling class, since they can be used to justify unity between bosses and workers in which class divisions can be presented as of secondary importance. For this reason, racism becomes institutionalised within the structures of society.

Racism varies in quality and degree, but its roots lie in capitalist competition. In his book **The German Ideology**, Marx summarised the impact of competition:

> Competition separates individuals from one another, not only the bourgeois but still more the workers, in spite of the fact that it brings them together. Hence it is a long time before these individuals can unite... Hence every organised power standing over against these isolated individuals, who live in conditions daily reproducing this isolation, can only be overcome after long struggles.[2]

Communism, *a classless society*, is the final stage of this struggle. The ending of competition, the withering away of the state and the eradication of racism are parts of this process. Racism would be incompatible with the needs of this new, classless society. Workers' power would proceed to uproot once and for all the material basis for racism: competition and racist institutions.

The transition from competition to workers' power is crucial: how can a divided working class be won to the struggle to overthrow capitalism and build a classless society?

Although capitalism forces workers to compete, it also forces them to work together, to cooperate in order to produce. In the process workers gain a sense of their common interests and the need to take common action to defend these.

The early utopian socialists saw workers as the *objects* of history: poor, exploited souls who would be far better off in a socialist society, a society to be achieved by means of moral persuasion, not class struggle. By contrast, Marx began with an analysis of capitalism, and identified a central contradiction: capitalism cannot survive without the wage-labour of the working class, but the working class has no interest in capitalism's continued existence. **The Communist Manifesto**, written at the beginning of 1848, sets out the results of this contradiction:

> The growing competition among the bourgeois, and the resulting commercial crises, make the wages of the workers even more fluctuating. The unceasing improvement of machinery, ever more rapidly developing, makes their livelihood more and more precarious; the collisions between individual workmen and individual bourgeois take more and more the character of collisions between two classes. Thereupon the workers begin to form combinations against the bourgeois; they club together in order to keep up the rate of wages; they found permanent associations in order to make provisions

beforehand for these occasional revolts.[3]

Marx describes the working class as the 'special and essential product' of modern history:

> The essential condition for the existence, and for the sway of the bourgeois class, is the formation and augmentation of capital: the condition for capital is wage-labour. Wage-labour rests exclusively on competition between the labourers. The advance of industry, whose involuntary promoter is the bourgeoisie, replaces the isolation of the labourers, due to competition, by their revolutionary combination, due to association. The development of modern industry, therefore, cuts from under its feet the very foundation on which the bourgeoisie produces and appropriates products. What the bourgeoisie therefore produces, above all, are its own grave-diggers. Its fall and the victory of the proletariat are equally inevitable.[4]

For Marx the industrial working class was not the passive object of history; it was a class in the process of becoming the *subject* of history, and he described it as 'the only really revolutionary class.'[5]

Marx thus advances two crucial propositions. First, the common conditions of exploitation which workers suffer forces them to form collective organisations in order to defend their shared interests against capital. Secondly, this struggle transforms the workers themselves, forming them into a united and selfconscious class oriented increasingly on the struggle against the capitalist state itself.

How do these two propositions apply to the struggle against racism?

In the first place, Marxists claim that white workers have a material interest in the liberation of black people from their oppression. This goes against the idea, shared by black nationalists and by many reformists, that white workers benefit from the existence of racism. It also seems to fly in the face of common sense. After all, white workers are typically better off than their black brothers and sisters, earning higher pay, doing better jobs, and living in better homes. So are we ignoring reality?

An American Marxist scholar, Albert Szymanski, set out to test two competing claims — the theory advocated by many liberal academics that white workers benefit from racism, and the Marxist analysis, according to which:

> ... racial antagonisms cause white and black workers to fight each other to the mutual detriment of both. The somewhat better jobs and

wages of white workers are not enough to make up for what they lose because of the lack of solidarity with black workers.[6]

Using census data Szymanski studied the relative earnings of black and white workers in the fifty states of the US. His findings completely refuted the idea that white workers benefit from racism. They were:

1. 'The higher black earnings relative to white, the higher white earnings relative to other Whites.'

2. 'The greater the discrimination against Third World people, [mainly Blacks, but also Hispanics] the higher the inequality among Whites.'

3. In 'those states with more than 12 per cent Third World people ... the more Third World people relative to Whites, the lower white earnings.'

4. 'The higher the proportion of Third World people in a state's population, the *more* inequality there is among Whites... the relatively poor Whites lose disproportionately from discrimination against Third World people compared to the better-paid Whites.'[7]

Szymanski concluded:

> It is clear that white working people do not gain economically by economic discrimination against Third World people... White workers appear to actually lose economically from racial discrimination. These results appear to support the Marxist theory... [8]

Szymanski also found support for the idea that white workers lose out because racism undermines working-class solidarity. Using the percentage of workers in unions as an indicator of the degree of solidarity, he found that 'the more intense racial discrimination is, the lower are the white earnings *because*... working-class solidarity' is weaker.[9]

Although Szymanski's study was of racism in the US, there is no reason to believe that the situation is any different in Britain.[10] It shows that *racism, because it divides the working class, is contrary to the interests of white workers*. White workers are worse off materially because of racism. It is therefore in their interest even in the narrowest of material terms, to fight racism.

This analysis also indicates whose interests racism serves. The more divided and therefore the weaker workers are, the stronger the capitalist class is and the larger its profits. *Racism, because it divides the working class, is in the interests of capital.*

The middle classes — the small businessmen, professionals and managers — are, because of their position in society, politically inconsistent. They tend to vacillate between the ruling class and the working class.

This is also true of their attitude to racism. In periods of social crisis, when the working class has been weakened, the middle class is capable of turning to racism and fascism *en masse*. They do so because racism seems to provide a means of protecting their collective interests. In Germany in the 1930s the middle classes turned to anti-semitism and provided the Nazis with their mass support. It is not impossible that in a similar period of social crisis this could happen in Britain as well.

Even that section of the middle class which opposes racism will not challenge the underlying material base — capitalism — on which it rests. Instead they tend towards moralistic ₄arguments and individual action rather than collective class action.

The only class which has a definite material interest in fighting and eradicating racism is the working class. Racism divides and weakens the working class. However, to say that is not to say that the majority of workers are at present anti-racist. This is clearly not so. The consciousness of workers is contradictory: they are influenced on the one hand by the ideas propagated by the ruling class, on the other by their experience of class struggle. Ideas of race, nationalism and individual competition pull one way; ideas of class, internationalism and collective action pull in the opposite direction.

The Italian Marxist Antonio Gramsci explained contradictory consciousness like this:

> The active man-in-the-mass has a practical activity but has no clear theoretical consciousness of his practical activity, which nonetheless involves understanding the world in so far as it transforms it. His theoretical consciousness can indeed be historically in opposition to his activity. One might almost say that he has two theoretical consciousnesses (or one contradictory consciousness): one which is implicit in his activity and which in reality unites him with all fellow-workers in the practical transformation of the real world; and one, superficially explicit or verbal, which he has inherited from the past and uncritically absorbed.
>
> The personality is strangely composite: it contains Stone Age elements and principles of a more advanced science, prejudices from all past

phases of history at the local level and intuitions of a future philosophy which will be that of a human race united the world over.[11]

When workers break from the old ways of thinking, from their acceptance of ruling class ideas, they do so because those ideas come into conflict with their new experience. The experience of struggle is particularly important because it rapidly leads to a conflict with a series of bourgeois ideas. Even the smallest strike quickly demonstrates the need for unity among workers. In the process, the old ideas of racist division become an encumbrance, and workers may reject them entirely.

Consciousness is not a fixed and static phenomenon. Periods of class struggle will tend to encourage ideas of class unity, while periods of passivity will tend to encourage racism. Nor is consciousness the same for every worker. Some workers will tend more towards socialism and a rejection of the dominant ideas of society, others to compliance and servility. The generally contradictory nature of this consciousness means that it is possible to be a class fighter *and* a racist. However, the most consistent class fighters, the socialists, are of necessity and by definition anti-racist.

The class struggle, therefore, tends to create conditions in which the divisions among workers can be broken down. If this is true in general, how much more true is it during a socialist revolution, in which the working class reaches for political power?

John Molyneux has suggested three reasons why the process of revolution would itself deal racism many powerful blows:

> First, because it is certain that black workers will themselves play a powerful and leading role in the revolution. Second, because unless unity is achieved between the decisive sections of the black and white working class (on the basis of total opposition to racism) the revolution cannot hope to achieve victory. Third, because a victorious, confident working class that has been through the enlightening experience of revolutionary struggle will feel no need for scapegoats. Building on this firm basis, a socialist society which unites workers as collective owners and controllers of production rather than dividing them... will steadily eliminate the last vestiges of racism.[12]

Revolutionary socialists, because they seek to achieve workers' power, which depends upon the unity of the working class, are the firmest and most consistent opponents of racism. Marx and Engels wrote in **The Communist Manifesto** that revolutionary socialists,

... are distinguished from the other working-class parties by this only:
1. In the national struggles of the proletarians of the different countries, they point out and bring to the front the common interests of the entire proletariat, independently of all nationality. 2. In the various stages of development which the struggle of the working class against the bourgeoisie has to pass through, they always and everywhere represent the interests of the movement as a whole.[13]

Thus, from the first, Marxists have seen internationalism as fundamental. This means not only rejecting and overcoming racist divisions in the world working class, but also divisions based on competing 'national interests'. For Marx, internationalism was linked to the practical and immediate problems of day-to-day class struggle. Working class unity was essential. Sectionalism, national chauvinism, sexism and racism were to be opposed, therefore, not as moral issues but because they were barriers in the way of class unity.

Marx rejected the old utopian slogan of 'the brotherhood of man', because its content was idealist and moralist. It is a mistake to see the employer and the press, the pulpit and the police as our 'brothers'. They act constantly and consistently against the interests of the working class, black and white. Instead Marx counterposed the slogan 'Workers of all nations unite', a slogan which expressed the interests of the workers as a class.

The reformist socialists of today share with the utopians a belief in socialism from above. They share a vision of peaceful change, of cooperation between classes rather than class conflict, of workers as the passive object and not the active subject of history. They also share a common understanding of racism. They see it as a moral issue, not a product of capitalism.

The major problem they then face is how to balance the real material demands of the capitalist system, which they want to tame rather than abolish, against this moral opposition to racism. How should they balance opposition to racism against the need to maintain electoral support, to win business approval for new investment, to prevent a threatened rebellion by a section of the state machine on which they depend? In such circumstances they will compromise — which is why the anti-racism of the reformists is always superficial.

The liberal and reformist opposition to racism is based on moral priorities. It is therefore *conditional* and *fallible*. The anti-racism of

Marxists is integral to the material necessities of the working class and the political imperatives of socialism. It is *fundamental* and *absolute*.

Anti-racism and Workers' Struggles

Marxism's identification of the working class as the central force in fighting racism is no mere act of faith, or theoretical abstraction. It rests on the fact that capitalism draws workers together from many different countries and backgrounds into a process of production where they are exploited together and can defend their interests only by forging collective organisation which overcomes racial or national differences among them. Again and again when workers have fought capital they have shown themselves able to break down these divisions, rejecting the racist ideas which keep them weak. There is space for only a couple of examples here, but they underline the importance that anti-racist traditions have for the labour movement even in countries with the most appalling histories of oppression and prejudice.

At the time of Marx's birth in 1818, there was in London a distinct revolutionary current, the followers of Thomas Spence, which involved a section of the working class. At the same time there were several thousand black people living in London, most of them descended from slaves. Among the leaders of this revolutionary current were at least two Blacks: William Davidson and Robert Wedderburn.[14]

Robert Wedderburn was born in Jamaica in 1762 and came to work in London as an artisan. He was a member of the working class and took part in the political life of the class. He was a noted speaker and pamphleteer. On one occasion he urged his supporters to break with a one-time 'fellow traveller', Henry Hunt, saying that 'his principles of Reform would not suit their purpose, which must be nothing short of a revolution.'[15]

One issue which Spence's followers raised was particularly dear to Wedderburn's heart: slavery. On one occasion he invited two black West Indian speakers to expose a missionary scheme sponsored by the Wesleyans. In 1824 he wrote an autiobiographical piece, **The Horrors of Slavery**, in which he detailed the flogging of his 70-year-old grandmother, which he had witnessed when he was about eleven years old.

Wedderburn smuggled revolutionary literature to slaves in Jamaica, arguing against the suggestion that they should petition for emancipation — 'For it is degrading to human nature to petition your oppressors' — and in favour of an annual one-hour strike. He envisaged a simultaneous revolution of poor white Europeans and black West Indian slaves.

Before his conviction and imprisonment for blasphemous libel, Wedderburn was organising lectures and debates three times a week, charging sixpence a head and attracting audiences of up to two hundred. Here is an account of one meeting in 1819:

> Wedderburn, who describes himself as *'The Offspring of an African'*, was *'highly gratified'* by the outcome of a debate on whether a slave had the right to kill a master. The question 'was decided in favour of the slave without a dissenting voice, by a numerous and enlightened assembly, who exultingly expressed their desire of hearing of another sable nation freeing itself by the dagger from the base tyranny of their Christian masters'; indeed, *'several gentlemen declared their readiness to assist them'*.[16]

Imagine the scene: a meeting of working-class Londoners listen to a black revolutionary who proposes that black slaves have a right to kill their white masters; they give him their enthusiastic support! And some people argue that British workers are *inherently* racist?

The Chartists, the first great workers' political movement, emerged in Britain in the late 1830s. By 1848 the most prominent leader of Chartism in London was another black man, William Cuffay. **The Times** attempted to ridicule the London Chartists by referring to them as 'the black man and his party'.[17]

Cuffay was born in Chatham, the son of a freed West Indian slave and the grandson of an African sold into slavery. When he could find a job he worked as a tailor. He was a revolutionary and rejected the 'moral force' wing of Chartism. At the 1848 convention he was given the job of organising the march which was to accompany the Chartists' great petition to parliament. The planned march panicked the ruling class: the queen was packed off to the Isle of Wight for her safety and royal carriages and other valuables removed from the palace. But they also prepared their armed forces, and these sufficiently impressed the Chartist leader Feargus O'Connor for him to call the march off.

Cuffay was later sentenced to transportation and died in Tasmania, aged 82. He spent twenty years in exile, many of them engaged in working-class agitation. In **The Times** report of his trial he was sneered at as 'half a "nigger".' Others had a different view. **Reynold's Political Instructor** wrote that he was:

> ...loved by his own order, who knew him and appreciated his virtues, ridiculed and denounced by a press that knew him not, and had no sympathy with his class, and banished by a government that feared him... Whilst integrity in the midst of poverty, whilst honour in the midst of temptation are admired and venerated, so long will the name of William Cuffay, a scion of Africa's oppressed race, be preserved from oblivion.[18]

One of the major political issues of the day was that of Ireland, and the Chartists identified fully with the struggle for Irish independence. Cuffay even argued that the stewards for the 1848 march should wear tricolour sashes and rosettes. The Chartists were prejudiced neither against Blacks nor against the Irish. Feargus O'Connor and Bronterre O'Brien, the Chartists' greatest leaders, were both Irish. O'Connor was an internationalist and argued that:

> ...the oppressed classes in England and Ireland must fight together and conquer together or continue to languish under the same burden and live in the same misery and dependence on the privileged and ruling class.[19]

Wedderburn, Davidson, O'Connor and Cuffay were examples of an important phenomenon. When workers fight they need the maximum unity: discriminating against individuals because of the colour or nationality becomes a definite disadvantage. Furthermore, when workers fight they select as leaders those most capable of guiding them in struggle. They do not have to be men, or speak with the right accent, or know who won the FA Cup in 1924. Women have often been prominent in the battles of the working class. Trotsky, the organiser of the Bolshevik insurrection of 1917, was a Jew.

The retreat of the British workers' movement from the fine traditions of the early nineteenth century is a reflection of the growth, after the defeat of Chartism in 1848, of a social layer wedded to the negotiation of class compromise within the framework of the existing system. *This* tradition reached its full flowering in the modern trade union bureaucracy and its political expression in the Labour Party. The reformists, by holding back workers' struggles, prevent the development of the kind of consciousness and confidence which can break down divisions. It is by building on the revolutionary tradition represented by the 'physical force' Chartists, and men like Wedderburn and Davidson that racism can be fought and beaten.

A second example of anti-racism in workers' struggles is provided by the American Congress of Industrial Organisations, the CIO. The history of American labour has been — for the most part — the history of two philosophies, two kinds of organisation. The AFL always concerned itself with protecting the privileged position of skilled workers. Since most Blacks were unskilled workers, this excluded most Blacks from membership. When black workers were allowed to join the AFL they were almost always recruited to a segregated branch of the organisation. The AFL defended racial discrimination, and gave trade unions a bad name among Blacks.

The syndicalists, on the other hand, aimed to organise all workers within a particular industry: skilled with unskilled, black with white. David Milton wrote of industrial unionism that it 'cannot be equated with revolution, but it required a degree of class interest, consciousness and organisational solidarity strong enough to withstand the bullets, spies, intimidation and coercive power wielded by the largest corporations in the country.'[20] Of necessity, therefore, the industrial unionists opposed racial and other forms of discrimination This was true of the Knights of Labor, who organised 60,000 black members when at their height in 1886;[21] it was true of the 'Wobblies', the Industrial Workers of the World; it was true of the CIO, formed in 1935, which resolved:

> *Whereas*, Employers constantly seek to split one group of workers from another, and thus to deprive them of their full economic strength, by arousing prejudices based on race, creed, color or nationality, and one of the most frequent weapons used by employers to accomplish this end is to create false contests between Negro and white workers; now therefore be it
>
> *Resolved*, that the CIO hereby pledges itself to uncompromising opposition to any form of discrimination, whether political or economic, based on race, color, creed or nationality.[22]

John L Lewis, the leader of the CIO, hired black organisers to help increase the number of black members. He also employed members of the Communist Party because of their 'special interest in the unity of black and white labor'.[23] The CIO's sympathetic attitude towards black workers paid off: by 1940 there were roughly 500,000 black trade unionists, mostly in CIO-affiliated unions.

The main reason for the growth of the CIO was that it organised, it fought and it won. Black and white workers benefitted materially from united action. In the steel industry, for instance, an intensive recruitment drive took the Steel Workers' Organising Committee to 550,000 members by 1937. In the process strikes were won, wages raised by one-third, working hours reduced and in some plants discrimination by management was stopped.[24] In 1940 the black president of a steelworkers' union Local (branch) told the press:

> Has the CIO played fair with us Negro workers? Well, look at the new clothes our children wear... See how the white and colored workers get along together since they started wearing the union buttons.[25]

Even the paper of the normally conservative Urban League had to admit:

> To the American Negro the coming of the CIO has been the most important historical experience in 75 years of struggle for a chance to live and achieve. This is true also for millions of white industrial workers, but it is true in double measure for the forgotten black workers of American history.[26]

As Daniel Guérin put it:

> The CIO, by virtue of its very existence, indirectly acted as a support and a bulwark for the black community as a whole, enabling it to consolidate its forces, pluck up the courage to formulate new demands, take a more independent attitude and prepare the ground for the mass struggles it has fought since then.[27]

The potential of the mass unions of the 1930s was, alas, never fully realised. The founders of the CIO were trade union bureaucrats like Lewis who were prepared to ally themselves with rank-and-file militants in order to organise industry. They remained, as trade union leaders, wedded firmly to a policy of class collaboration. The bitter fruits of this approach were harvested during the Second World War, when the bureaucrats strove to contain a growing surge of rank-and-file discontent against the sacrifices and speed-up demanded of them. The most vicious opponents of any kind of strike action proved to be the American Communist Party, pledged to devote all its efforts to sustaining the wartime alliance between Russia and America.

In this atmosphere of shopfloor discontent and feverish nationalism, many white workers turned on the Blacks flooding into the war industries. A rash of 'hate strikes' aimed at Blacks undermined the unity forged in the late 1930s and laid the basis for the racial divisions at work against which groups such as DRUM rebelled in the 1960s. The bureaucrats of the CIO soon looked little different from their counterparts in the old racist craft unions of the AFL, and the two federations fused in 1955.

The lesson of the CIO and Chartism is clear. When workers combine against the employer they begin to reject racism. Moreover, it is the fight, and the material benefits which it brings, that draw black workers (and white workers) into active participation in the unions.

However, a high level of class struggle is not sufficient to break the hold of racism on white workers. If the force for class collaboration within the workers' movement — above all, the trade union bureaucracy and the reformist parties — are allowed to triumph, then the old divisions will be restored. The revolutionary opponents of racism must organise to win the mass of workers to their ideas. But how?

THE PARTY AND THE OPPRESSED

Marx believed that workers should form a party of their own. He conceived a broad party of class-conscious workers, whose growth and political development would depend on the impact of class struggles from below — a spontaneous process. Events since Marx's day have shown that building a workers' party is more complicated than he anticipated.

By 1914 the German Social Democratic Party (SPD) was receiving more than four and a half million votes in parliamentary elections. It had more than one million members, produced ninety daily papers, and ran mass trade unions, cooperatives, sports and social clubs, a youth organisation and a women's organisation. The party had a 'maximum programme', which called for the overthrow of capitalism and enabled it to claim allegiance to revolutionary Marxism. But this was hermetically sealed from its minimum programme, a series of demands which could be achieved within capitalism and which enabled it to be reformist in practice. The real nature of the SPD was exposed in August 1914, when its leaders voted for 'war credits' to support German militarism in the First World

War. It was exposed again when its leaders were responsible for the murders of the two revolutionary socialist leaders Rosa Luxemburg and Karl Liebknecht.

The SPD was no isolated example. In Britain leading trade unionists worked with men such as Keir Hardie to form a Labour Party clearly committed to peaceful reform. In Russia the Mensheviks, for many years the largest workers' party, participated in the Provisional government set up after the revolution of February 1917, then attempted to destroy the workers' revolution of the following October.

These big 'workers' parties' were led by people who had a material interest in preserving capitalism. The British trade union bureaucrat was a prime example. Separated from his old workmates, he acquired a privileged existence beyond their control. He administered their association and negotiated their level of exploitation. Such an important and rewarding position was threatened by the prospect of mass upheavals, from which the union bureaucrat could gain nothing and lose all. Similarly the Labour members of parliament with whom the union leaders allied. In Germany the SPD was almost a 'state within a state'. The livelihood of many hundreds of officials depended on stability and the party's continued well-being.

These reformist leaders base themselves upon the normally passive majority of the working class. When a major class battle develops — a mass strike occurs and workers' councils are formed — there is the potential for revolution. But it is only a possibility if a party exists which can organise the politically advanced workers in opposition to the influence of the reformist leaders of the labour movement. Otherwise, lacking determined leadership capable of releasing the creativity of the class, the majority of workers will avoid a decisive confrontation. A minority may fight, only to be suppressed.

Revolutionary socialists, however, do not aim to impose their politics on the majority, but to organise the advanced workers in order to *convince* the majority of the need for revolution. Socialism is the self-emancipation of the working class, not the act of a minority.

This party of advanced workers is not the broad party which Marx envisaged. It is a vanguard party of the type that Lenin helped to build. It is *consciously* built by politically conscious workers and other socialists. Such a party must be constructed in advance of major confrontations. It cannot just proclaim itself in the midst of the battle and, without any preparation, expect to provide a credible alternative to the reformist leadership.

It is possible to build this party even in times when there is a low level of class struggle by demonstrating, to a politically conscious minority of workers, that revolutionary socialist politics are superior to those of the reformists. This is not merely a matter of exposing and denouncing the reformists; it also means that revolutionary socialists must be involved in all the limited and partial struggles of the day. The revolutionary socialist gains the respect of his or her fellow workers by being the most determined and effective fighter against exploitation and oppression — and therefore of necessity against racism. Thus there is no conflict between the immediate need to fight racism and the ultimate struggle for socialist revolution. On the contrary they reinforce each other.

Tribunes of the People

In 1902 Lenin wrote **What is to be done?** as a polemic against the 'economist' current within the Russian Marxist movement. The 'economists' believed that socialists should concentrate on factory agitation; that once workers were spurred into action over economic issues they would learn, through their own experience of struggle, of the need to raise political demands and engage in political struggles. Lenin argued that it was necessary to make a distinction between trade union consciousness and socialist consciousness. The immediate economic struggle developed only trade union consciousness. Because trade unionism was compatible with bourgeois society, however, and because trade union struggles did not normally raise a vision of a socialist society, 'trade unionist politics of the working class are precisely bourgeois politics of the working class'.[28]

Writing before the great upheavals which culminated in the 1905 revolution, Lenin underestimated the potential for workers to develop a socialist consciousness in the course of major class struggle. Nevertheless, his argument is enormously important, particularly for anyone attempting to build a revolutionary party in times when the level of class struggle is relatively low. Socialist or 'class political' consciousness,

...can be brought to the workers *only from without*, that is, only from outside of the economic struggle, from outside of the sphere of relations between workers and employers. The sphere from which alone it is possible to obtain this knowledge is the sphere of relationships between *all* the classes and strata and the state and the government, the sphere of the interrelations between *all* the classes.[29]

The need for workers' unity could be learned from direct experience of workers' struggle, said Lenin, but the need to support the struggles of oppressed groups required the intervention of socialist argument. For this reason Lenin argued that revolutionary socialists had to be more than just trade unionists; they had to be 'tribunes of the people',

...able to react to every manifestation of tyranny and oppression, no matter where it takes place, no matter what stratum or class of people it affects; ...able to generalise all these manifestations to produce a single picture of police violence and capitalist exploitation; ...able to take advantage of every event, however small, in order to explain his socialist convictions and his democratic demands to *all*, in order to explain to *all* and everyone the world-historic significance of the proletariat's struggle for emancipation.[30]

Lenin's argument contained two interlinked propositions.

First, the need for workers to identify with the struggles of the oppressed. Even if these were not of immediate and direct concern to workers, they were battles with the enemies of the working class, capable of weakening the power of the ruling class, if only to a small degree. Lenin argued that workers should support the student movement in Russia in 1899. Later he urged support for national minorities opposing the domination of the Russian state.

Lenin's support for the struggle of the oppressed was not conditional on their pursuing the correct strategy. Indeed he argued:

To imagine that socialist revolution is *conceivable* without revolts by small nations in the colonies and Europe, without revolutionary outbursts by a section of the bourgeoisie *with all its prejudices*, without a movement of the politically non-conscious proletariat and semi-proletarian masses against oppression by the landowners, the church, and the monarchy, against national oppressions, etc — to imagine all this is to *repudiate socialist revolution*. So one army lines up in one place and says, 'We are for socialism', and another somewhere else, and says 'We are for imperialism', and that will be a social revolution! ... Whoever expects a 'pure' social revolution will *never* live to see it.[31]

In Britain, and even more so in America, the struggle of black people against oppression has sometimes moved in a nationalist or separatist direction. Socialists should defend the right of black people to choose to organise independently, against their oppression. This should not, however, inhibit criticism of the tactics used.

The second element of Lenin's argument is of fundamental importance. He argued that a victory for the working class would be a victory for all oppressed groups. Workers' power would end the power of the police who whipped the students; it would free the oppressed nations; it would stop all the racist deportations. Indeed, *only* the working class had the power to destroy the state which was responsible for these and many other forms of oppression.

Lenin's starting point, therefore, was the need to unite the whole working class in the fight against *all* forms of exploitation and oppression. This is quite different from the proposal for a 'rainbow alliance'. Lenin was concerned to show that all the exploited and the oppressed have a common interest in the overthrow of the capitalist state. The 'rainbow alliance' assumes the continuation of the state and seeks an alliance only to gain resources or concessions.

Just as capitalism divides worker from worker, it divides one section of the oppressed from another. There is no natural or necessary unity of the oppressed. There were gays in Nazi Germany who supported Hitler in his oppression of the Jews. There are West Indians in Britain who are against Asians, and vice versa. Looking down upon someone less fortunate than yourself can provide some relief from one's own oppression.

In the US, Jesse Jackson tolerates anti-semites among his leading supporters. In Britain Haringey council is openly anti-gay. In both these cases reformist politicians have made concessions to prejudice in order to gain electoral advantage. Revolutionary socialists make no such concessions. They are not interested in elections but in unity for the struggle against capitalism. They must therefore oppose every form of prejudice and act as 'tribunes of the people' in fighting every form of oppression.

Socialists should urge workers to support the oppressed, the oppressed to support workers, and all to fight for socialism. This is in the material interests of workers and in the material interests of the oppressed.

A united party

Lenin's position in fighting for the widest and fullest working-class unity was criticised at the time by the General Union of Jewish Workers, the Bund, which organised the Jewish workers of Lithuania, Poland and parts of Russia. Because of the uneven development of capitalism, these workers happened to be more politically advanced than most. The Bund was formed before the main Russian Social Democratic Party but joined it at its inception in 1898. In the early days the various units of the party, including the Bund, were forced by Tsarist oppression to develop in isolation from one another and from the virtually non-existent party centre. By the time of the party's second congress, in 1903, it had become clear that the Bund had moved in a separatist direction.

The leaders of the Bund argued that there was a distinct Jewish nation, with its own working class, and that the Bund was its sole legitimate representative. They advocated 'cultural autonomy' for all national groups. Each 'nation' should be empowered to tax its members and should have autonomy in cultural matters such as education. Connected with this, they argued that the Bund should have the right to determine policies specifically relating to Jews, and that the party should be constituted as a federation of national groups.

Lenin, however, argued that 'the idea that the Jews form a separate nation is... absolutely untenable scientifically', and that this 'Zionist idea' was 'essentially reactionary'. All over Europe, he said, political liberty had been accompanied by the political emancipation of the Jews, and this had been followed by their progressive assimilation with the surrounding population. It was the reactionaries who opposed assimilation and attempted to perpetuate the isolation of the Jews. The Bund, he argued, were wrong to 'legitimise Jewish isolation, by propagating the idea of the Jewish "nation".' This encouraged 'a spirit hostile to assimilation, the spirit of the "ghetto",' which ran counter to the interests of the Jewish workers.[32]

Lenin particularly opposed the proposed application of 'cultural autonomy' to the school system. It would mean that school students would be divided according to 'nationality' and educated alongside others from their own 'nation'. This meant, he said, 'pursuing or supporting bourgeois nationalism, chauvinism and clericalism'. In

Lenin's view 'the interest of democracy in general, and the interests of the working class in particular, demand the *mixing* of the children of *all* nationalities in *uniform* schools in each locality.'[33] In a later article on the schools question he added:

> The class-conscious workers combat all national oppression and all national privileges, but they do not confine themselves to that. They combat all, even the most refined, nationalism, and advocate not only the unity, but also the *amalgamation* of the workers of *all* nationalities in the struggle against reaction and against bourgeois nationalism in all its forms. Our task is not to segregate nations, but to unite the workers of all nations. Our banner does not carry the slogan 'national culture' but *international culture*, which unites all the nations in a higher socialist unity, and the way to which is already being paved by the international amalgamation of capital.[34]

At the 1903 congress Lenin supported the main speakers against the Bund: Martov, who later became the leader of the Mensheviks and Trotsky. They were both Jews, and this in itself helped to undermine the Bund's claim to be the sole representative of the Jewish working class.

The argument put forward against the Bund was that the aim of the party was to unite workers to overthrow the Tsarist state. Organising Jewish and non-Jewish workers separately in each town could only hinder this. It would for instance make it more difficult to counter anti-semitism if Jewish workers were not in the same organisations as the rest. If the party was to be effective in organising all workers, it had to be united itself. This implied centralism, not federalism. The party as a whole determined its programme, and every unit of the party—including the Bund—should apply the programme in its particular area of work. The rules of the party applied to every committee and member of the party and there could be no exceptions for the Bund.

The Bund lost the vote and left the congress. Although its representatives made appearances at subsequent congresses, it retained a separate, autonomous existence.

On 2 November 1917, only a week after the Bolsheviks had taken control of Petrograd in the October insurrection, the Council of Peoples Commissars published its decree on the rights of Russian nationalities.[35] For Jews the decree meant the removal of numerous anti-semitic restrictions and the establishment of full freedom and equality. Despite this, the Bund joined the Mensheviks in opposing the revolution. It aligned itself with the forces of counter-revolution, some of which were prepared to use anti-semitism, and even *pogroms*, to mobilise the most politically backward working people against the revolution. The Council of People's Commissars responded to reports of anti-semitism by instructing deputies to the soviets to take 'uncompromising measures to tear the anti-semitic movement out by the roots'.[36]

The revolution led, initially, to a flowering of Jewish culture, with the Yiddish language used in newspapers, theatres and schools. There is also evidence, however, that with the removal of restrictions, Jews flocked into Russian schools, and began reading Russian papers in larger numbers.[37] There is no contradiction between these two trends;[37] the revolution made both possible. In the early days, the tentative steps towards assimilation occurred on a purely voluntary basis.

The situation in Russia today is, of course, very different. The Jewish religion is suppressed, emigration is severely restricted, and Jews are discriminated against in certain jobs. Nathan Weinstock, in his book **Zionism: False Messiah**, argues that: 'Jewish self-awareness in the USSR thrives not on nationalistic consciousness, nor on a religious feeling, not even on Jewish pride. The breeding ground is solely the bitterness generated by bureaucratic repression'.[38] The oppression of Jews in modern Russia is merely the most publicised example of a broader phenomenon: Russian chauvinism and the oppression of national minorities in general.

The transformation in official attitudes occurred under Stalin. The concept of 'Socialism in one country' marked a break with the internationalism of Marx and Lenin. Lenin had argued that the slogan of 'national culture' was 'a bourgeois... fraud', and that 'our slogan is... international culture'; Stalin argued that under the dictatorship of the proletariat, culture is 'socialist in content and national in form'.[39]

In practice 'national culture' meant *Russian* national culture. A decree of May 1934 condemned all previous accounts of Russian history and rehabilitated words such as 'homeland' and 'patriotism'. The glorious history of the Russian people was traced back to the third millenium BC, and 'nation' replaced 'class' as the most important historical concept. Nigel Harris, in his book **Beliefs in**

Society, argues:

> Inevitably, since the basic historic unit was now identified not by its role in the social structure but by its ethnic descent, racialism appeared, for only 'the blood' could identify who was part of the heroic people.[40]

Nationalism (and underlying it, racism) is used in much the same way today in Russia as it is in Britain, to bind the majority of workers to the ruling class. This is itself a reflection of the class nature of Russian society — not socialist, no longer a workers' state, but a form of capitalism where the bureaucracy maintains itself as a ruling class by means of its control of the state.

REVOLUTIONARIES AND ANTI-RACISM TODAY

The argument in this book has been based on several propositions: that racism is a product of capitalist society; that racism is against the interests of the working class; that the unity of workers in struggle needs to be central if we are to undermine racism; that the achievement of socialism and the eradication of racism require the building of a revolutionary party. This is the argument put forward by revolutionary socialists. How, in practice, have these general propositions related to actual struggle?

For the past twenty years the Socialist Workers Party (SWP) has been the major revolutionary socialist organisation in Britain. The SWP is committed to a number of general principles which are published, each week, in the party's newspaper **Socialist Worker**. These include:

> We oppose racism and imperialism. We oppose all immigration controls. We support the right of black people and other oppressed groups to organise their own defence. We support all genuine national liberation movements... The struggle for socialism is part of a world-wide struggle. We campaign for solidarity with workers in other countries. We oppose everything which turns workers from one country against those from other countries.

How have these principles affected the practice of the SWP?

Since 1945 agitation against black immigration has provided the main focus for racist movements in Britain. The issue of immigration has therefore provided a major test for those who oppose racism. In 1968, when the movement in support of Enoch Powell's racist outbursts grew rapidly, most socialists found themselves isolated. Some kept their heads down, other buckled under the pressure, following Labour's lead in arguing *for* immigration controls. Members of the International Socialists, the SWP's forerunner, were expected to answer the racists' lies and argue that immigration controls would not assist the working class. In some cases this was achieved only with the loss of popularity and party influence.

In the London docks there was, at the time, only one member of the International Socialists. On the day of the racist strike and march in support of Powell he made a lone protest against this action, in the face of bitter and spiteful opposition from other dockers. His protest won him few friends — but it demonstrated that revolutionary socialists, unlike most of the reformists, do not back down under pressure from racists.

At the same time **Socialist Worker** issued an appeal to other socialist groups for unity, arguing that the feeble and spineless response of the traditional leadership of the left demonstrated the need for a new socialist organisation. This appeal met with little response from other left groups, but many individuals radicalised by the student and workers' struggles of the late 1960s were drawn towards the International Socialists because of its support for unity against the racists.

In 1976 there was again a massive anti-immigrant campaign during which Powell and the fascists created a climate of race hatred which led directly to at least three racists murders. **Socialist Worker** responded with the headline 'They're welcome here', followed by five straightforward arguments that could be used in every workplace. This was reproduced in leaflet form; tens of thousands of these were distributed outside factories and handed out in shopping centres. Stickers, posters and badges were produced to support the campaign. Though it was impossible to compete with the mass media, the campaign gave many socialists and black people the confidence to stand against the rising tide of racism.

In 1976, unlike 1968, there was a militant response from young Blacks, particularly in Southall, the scene of one of the racist murders. Demonstrations were called, mainly by Asian organisations, and the International Socialists gave full support. One was particularly memorable. A National Front sympathiser persisted in breaking the Race Relations law by putting up a sign outside his house which read: 'For Sale to an English family'. Some enterprising members of the International Socialists removed the sign. It was ceremoniously burnt by supporters of the Southall Youth Movement during an anti-racist demonstration.

The anti-racist campaigns of 1976 paved the way for the Anti Nazi League.

By the mid-1970s the National Front was able to mobilise large and intimidating marches through mainly black areas. Their supporters were openly assaulting Blacks and 'reds', and breaking up liberal as well as socialist meetings. The 16.2 per cent of the vote won by their national organiser, Martin Webster, in the West Bromwich by-election of 1976 indicates their electoral appeal. They were making headway in several trade unions, including the railworkers' and the postal workers'.

At first opposition to the Nazi NF was *ad hoc* and local. A typical chain of events was that the Front would call a march; the Communist Party, through some committee or other, would mount a counter-demonstration, which went as far away from the Nazis as possible; meanwhile SWP members would try to get as close as possible in order to harass the Nazi NF march and try to reduce its impact.

Two events in 1977 helped transform this situation. First there was the Greater London Council election, in which the NF received 119,000 votes and threatened to replace the Liberals as the third party of British politics. They were becoming an electoral threat to the Labour Party. Since they were taking Labour votes, this might enable the Tories to win some marginal constituencies. For this reason, in addition to genuine opposition to the racists and fascists, some leading members of the Labour Party were more willing to work with the SWP.

The second event was at Lewisham in August 1977, where the SWP and local black youth joined forces to mobilise 5000 anti-fascists against a march by the NF. Despite a massive police presence, the racists were prevented from marching. This undoubtedly boosted the reputation of the SWP, at least on the left.

The SWP approached Ernie Roberts, then an assistant general secretary of the engineering union and later a Labour member of parliament, and Peter Hain, the anti-apartheid activist, with a view to launching the Anti Nazi League as a united front against the fascists. Several hundred 'notables', ranging from eminent professors and members of parliament to football club managers and pop stars, sponsored its founding statement. These 'notables' (none of them Tories) were never allowed to determine the policies of the ANL, and some of them subsequently withdrew, but they did boost the ANL's credibility, and make it possible to mobilise tens of thousands of young people and trade unionists.

The ANL succeeded because it combined mass propaganda against racism — especially the carnivals organised in conjunction with Rock Against Racism — with militant action on the streets. Militancy alone would not have isolated the NF Nazis from their base among sections of workers, the middle classes and young people. Propaganda alone would not have prevented them from mobilising and motivating their supporters and raw recruits. The ANL made it possible to gather new anti-racist activists and new resources both for anti-racist propaganda and to oppose the NF on the streets.

The success of the Anti Nazi League can be measured in two ways.

First, it crippled the National Front. In the 1979 general election the NF received a derisory 1.3 per cent of the votes cast in the constituencies where it stood candidates. Demoralised, it split into three warring groups. In the 1981 GLC elections the combined Nazi vote averaged 2.1 per cent, compared with the 5.7 per cent it had received in 1977. Their support in the unions virtually disappeared, and in some — including the National Union of Railwayworkers — they were banned. Their marches, when they held them, were small and pathetic.

Second, the ANL was responsible for the biggest demonstrations against racism that Britain had seen since the Second World War. The carnivals drew up to 100,000 people each time, with 50,000 on the marches which preceded them. By the middle of 1979 at least nine million ANL leaflets had been distributed and 750,000 badges sold. This meant that in schools and workplaces up and down the country the balance of the argument shifted against the racists. This in turn had an impact on the Labour Party, which became far more concerned to appear anti-racist.

This is a record of which the SWP is understandably proud. The party initiated the ANL and provided its driving force. The ANL organising secretary, Paul Holborow, was a leading member of the SWP. So were nearly all its full-time staff and key local activists. The last major confrontation between the ANL and the Nazi NF was in Southall in April 1979. The police Special Patrol Group, defending the NF, brutally attacked many anti-Nazi demonstrators and killed teacher Blair Peach, who was a member of the SWP. His murder highlighted the commitment of revolutionary socialists to the fight against racism.

In the first half of 1987, as this book is being written, there are no major national campaigns against racism; but there are many smaller ones: defence campaigns for the victims of police racism, attempts to prevent deportations, and such like. It is of course important to support the demonstrations called by these campaigns, but socialists have a particular responsibility: to argue that such campaigns should be directed towards workplaces and trade union branches. First because that is where workers are collectively organised. Twenty people behind a union banner make more impact that twenty individuals. The more successful campaigns against deportation orders, for example that in support of Mohammed Idrish in 1985-6, have had significant trade union backing. Secondly, because if we are to undermine racism then the workplace is the best place to begin. That is where militants come into contact with workers, and where workers are more likely to think in terms of collective rather than individual interests.

Much of the work of countering racism is mundane, low-key and unglamorous: countering racist jokes, exposing media lies and such like. Occasionally a call for action finds a response. For instance in 1984 workers at BL's Longbridge plant in Birmingham came out on strike in support of a black worker, Zedekiah Mills, who had hit a racist foreman after being subject to prolonged racist abuse. In 1985 half the night shift at Ford's Dagenham plant came out on strike following the distribution of a 'joke' racist questionnaire in the plant. Later that year teachers from seventy schools in inner London joined an unofficial strike against racist attacks on school students. At the beginning of 1986 civil servants took strike action against the ethnic monitoring of welfare claimants.

Anti-racist strikes have become more common. Whether or not such strikes are possible depends upon the level of confidence and organisation in the workplace — something which is not just a matter of chance, but is affected by the activity of militants in organising not just against racism but over everyday issues such as pay and conditions. In the short term, anti-racist action in the workplace has a profound impact on the confidence of racists to organise. In the long term it is part of the creation of a united working-class movement which can defend *all* its members.

Many battles remain to be won, however, for not all socialists welcome such powerful demonstrations of anti-racism.

In 1985 the Labour-controlled council in Islington, North London, had a reputation as left-wing. It even made the telling of anti-Irish jokes a disciplinary offence. In one of its offices there was a group of hardened racists who had systematically harassed black workers. When there was a formal protest, the council refused to sack the individuals concerned; they were merely transferred. When the leader of the racists appeared in her new office, she was asked by fellow workers to give an undertaking not to persist with her racist behaviour. When she refused they walked out on strike, and the strike spread to other members of the Islington branch of NALGO.

What was the response of the left-wing council? To congratulate their workers for displaying such unity against the racists? Not at all. The chairperson of the council's personnel committee said the workers' action was 'harassment, albeit of a different kind'.[41] The council stuck it out and forced the strikers to back down. The strike was not in vain, however. Though the racists kept their jobs, they were isolated and less effective as a result of the strike against them.

The strike, vehemently opposed by the council, was supported by the SWP and some members of the Labour Party. It shows the difference between the two traditions of fighting racism: bureaucratic anti-racism allowed the racist to keep her job despite her refusal to change her racist behaviour; anti-racism 'from below' led to a magnificent display of class unity.

These concrete examples of the SWP's involvement in the struggle against racism are, in themselves, modest enough. Nevertheless they show how revolutionary socialist politics provides the basis for consistent opposition to racism.

REFORM OR REVOLUTION

We have argued that racism is a product of capitalist society. It can be understood and successfully opposed only on this basis. It has not always existed, nor need it continue to exist. Our conclusion is that if we are to uproot racism it is necessary to destroy capitalism.

Furthermore, in the process of conducting a systematic struggle against capitalism it is necessary to attack and undermine every division within the working class, including, most important, racism.

The separatists provide no solution. They can oppose racism. They can oppose capitalism. But, alone, they cannot eradicate capitalism and so are forced to accept the continued existence of racism. If they move towards revolution, they must move towards united class struggle and away from separatism. If not they must accept their increasing irrelevance, or move towards reformism. This has been the experience in America, and, to a lesser extent, in Britain.

The choice remains one of reform or revolution. But the reformists, because their opposition to capitalism is inconsistent, must necessarily be inconsistent in opposing racism. They do not like racism, but they support immigration controls. They help to maintain a police force which is thoroughly racist. They defend an economic system, which, in its ever deeper crises, is constantly reinforcing racism. They cannot abolish racism; they tolerate it; and, in practice, they encourage its development.

The alternative — for anti-racists, the only real alternative — is revolution. The aim of revolutionaries is socialism. Their practice is one of uncompromising resistance to capitalism and relentless struggle against racism.

Today the ideas of revolutionary socialism are those of a minority. But capitalism constantly breeds abnormal conditions, its inbuilt tendencies towards boom and slump forcing workers to organise and fight to defend their interests. It is in mass struggles, when workers move onto the offensive, uniting across the racial, sexual, national, and sectional boundaries that divide them, that revolutionaries can win a wider audience for their ideas.

Such struggles are rare in the Britain of the late 1980s, though the crisis of the local, and indeed the world ruling class makes future social explosions inevitable. For the present, revolutionaries have the vital task of welding together the Marxist political organisation which will be indispensible in the class battles ahead. In particular this means building a socialist alternative to reformism. It means challenging the traditions of class collaboration which have kept workers weak and disunited. Only by creating such a party can we ensure that Labour's record of betrayal and capitulation does not shape the future as well as the past. Only then can we ensure that the magnificent potential of workers is realised and that all forms of exploitation and oppression are swept away.

Suggested further reading

Peter Fryer's **Staying Power** (Pluto, London 1984) is an excellent history of black people in Britain. James Walvin's **Passage to Britain** (Penguin, Harmondsworth 1984) provides an account of immigration in British history. Zig Layton-Henry's **The Politics of Race in Britain** (Allen and Unwin, London 1984) is a useful survey covering the past fifty years, while Paul Gordon considers the major institutions of state racism in **White Law** (Pluto, London 1983).

Abram Leon's **The Jewish Question** (Pathfinder, New York 1970) is a first-rate summary of Jewish history from a Marxist perspective. Eric Williams' **Capitalism and Slavery** (Deutsch, London 1964) is a classical Marxist interpretation of slavery in the New World.

C L R James' contributions on the subject are to be found in a variety of publications, including **A History of Negro Revolt** (Race Today, London 1985), which was first published in 1938. Of all the accounts of black resistance written by participants, **The Autobiography of Malcolm X** (Penguin, Harmondsworth 1965) is probably the most important. A valuable though dry account of Blacks in American history is to be found in Philip Foner, **Organized Labor and the Black Worker** (International Publishers, New York 1974). On DRUM there is James Geschwender's **Class, Race and Worker Insurgency** (Cambridge 1977). **Detroit: I do mind dying**, by Dan Georgakas and Martin Surkin (St Martins Press, New York 1975) is unfortunately not easily available outside the US.

Chris Harman's excellent article, 'The Summer of 1981: A post-riot analysis' (**International Socialism**, number 2:14, Autumn 1981) is still available; further valuable political analyses are to be found in Leon Trotsky, **On Black Nationalism and Self-Determination** (Pathfinder, New York 1978) and V I Lenin, **On the Jewish Question** (International Publishers, New York 1974).

When in print, these books are available from Bookmarks' mail order service, 265 Seven Sisters Road, Finsbury Park, London N4 2DE, England. Write for an up-to-date booklist.

Notes

Chapter 1: THE ROOTS OF RACISM
1.   C L R James, **Modern Politics** (Detroit 1973) page 124.
2.   Frank M Snowden, **Before Color Prejudice** (Harvard University Press, Cambridge Massachusetts 1983) page 70.
3.   Ruth Benedict, **Race and Racism** (Routledge and Kegan Paul, London 1942) page 5.
4.   Anne Rogers argues, in 'The Roots of Racism' in **Socialist Worker Review**, number 82, December 1985, that Saint Augustine, several Roman emperors, and Hannibal were certainly African and probably black. She adds that such was the 'race blindness' of most ancient civilisations that it is impossible for us to discern the racial characteristics of certain leading historical figures.
5.   Snowden, page 63. See also Frank M Snowden, **Blacks in Antiquity: Ethiopians in the Graeco-Roman Experience** (Harvard University Press, Cambridge Massachusetts 1976) pages 182-3.
6.   James Walvin, **Black and White: The Negro and English Society 1555-1945** (Allen Lane, London 1973) page 2.
7.   Walvin, **Black and White**, page 9.
8.   Acts of the Privy Council of England, n.s. xxvi, pages 16-17, quoted in Peter Fryer, **Staying Power: The History of Black People in Britain** (Pluto Press, London 1984) page 10.
9.   Fryer, page 10.
10.   Walvin, **Black and White**, page 25.
11.   James, page 124.
12.   Karl Marx, **Capital** (Lawrence and Wishart, London 1954) page 226.
13.   Fryer, page 149.
14.   Walvin, **Black and White**, page 167.
15.   For instance Moses married a Kushite; see Snowden (1983), page 44.
16.   Cedric Dover, 'The Racial Philosophy of Jehuda Halevi' in **Phylon**, number 13, page 318.
17.   G E M de Ste Croix, **Class Struggles in the Ancient Greek World** (Duckworth, London 1981) page 420.
18.   As late as 1542 they legislated against enslavement of the Indians.

19. Eric Williams, **Capitalism and Slavery** (Deutsch, London 1983) page 18.
20. Williams, page 19. Later, he says, 'its origin can be explained in three words: in the Caribbean, Sugar; on the mainland, Tobacco and Cotton' (page 23). Williams' main purpose was to demonstrate the important contribution which slavery made to the development of British capitalism. Among others, the Barclay family—founders of Barclays Bank—prospered enormously from their investment in the slave trade (Fryer, page 46).
21. Fryer, page 146.
22. Morgan Godwyn, **The Negro's and Indians Advocate** (1680) page 61, quoted in Fryer, page 146. See also **Nothing but the Same Old Story: The Roots of Anti-Irish Racism** (Information on Ireland, London 1984), page 44.
23. Fryer, page 153.
24. Quoted in Fryer, page 159. Long's three-volume **History of Jamaica** was first published in 1774.
25. Williams, page 168.
26. Quoted in Fryer, page 211. The resolution was passed at a meeting of workers organised by Sheffield radicals in 1794.
27. Williams, page 210.
28. F D Lugard, **The Dual Mandate in British West Africa** (Blackwood, London 1922), quoted in Fryer, page 186.
29. For instance the massacre in 1865 of 439 free Jamaicans by forces under the command of General Eyre caused an enormous storm in Britain. He was supported by Ruskin, Tennyson, Dickens and Carlyle, and condemned by Mill, Huxley, Spencer and Darwin. It was in this period that **The Times** alleged that Britons had been deceived by the humanitarians into believing that 'the world was made for Sambo, and that the sale of sugar was to sweeten Sambo's existence' (quoted in Walvin, **Black and White**, page 172).
30. Quoted in Fryer, page 166.
31. Quoted in Fryer, page 181.
32. Quoted in Michael Banton, **Race Relations** (Tavistock, London 1967) page 42.
33. George L Mosse, **Towards the Final Solution** (Dent, London 1978) page 66.
34. Quoted in James Walvin, **Passage to Britain** (Penguin, Harmondsworth 1984) page 40.
35. Hal Draper, **Karl Marx's Theory of Revolution**, volume 2 (Monthly Review, New York 1978) page 68.
36. Walvin, **Passage**, page 42
37. Fryer, page 182.
38. Walvin, **Passage**, page 24.
39. E P Thompson, **The Making of the English Working Class** (Penguin, Harmondsworth 1968) page 469.
40. Walvin, **Passage**, page 49.
41. Joanna Rollo, 'History of Immigration' in **International Socialism**, number 1:96 (March 1977)—hereafter referred to as **ISJ**.
42. Karl Marx and Frederick Engels, **Articles on Britain** (Progress, Moscow 1975, page 161).

43. Thompson, page 480. He also notes: 'It is not the friction but the relative ease with which the Irish were absorbed into the working-class communities which is remarkable.'

44. Walvin, **Passage**, page 58.

45. Thompson, page 474.

46. Rollo, in 1:96, page 18.

47. Walvin, **Passage**, page 54.

48. Letter from Marx to Meyer and Vogt on 9 April 1870, in Marx and Engels, **Selected Correspondence**, quoted in Draper, volume 2, page 67 (Marx's italics). Marx and Engels also considered the similar, but more complicated, situation in America, where the bourgeoisie could take advantage of successive waves of immigrants, each from different countries, each competing with each other. In America the Irishman might be despised by the old English settlers, but he in turn could look down on the east Europeans, and all could look down on the Blacks, only recently released from slavery. See Draper, volume 2, pages 68-70.

49. Abram Leon, **The Jewish Question: A Marxist Interpretation** (Pathfinder, New York 1970).

50. Leon, page 81.

51. Leon, page 130.

52. Leon, pages 133 and 137.

53. Leon, pages 146-178.

54. In some places Jews survived in fringe occupations such as peddlars, pawnbrokers and second-hand dealers. In central Europe this was the period of the ghetto, special taxes, humiliating costumes and distinctive badges bearing the wheel emblem. Jews either fled, assimilated or lived a life of misery. See Leon, pages 82-3 and 153-4.

55. Leon, page 214.

56. Leon, page 204.

57. Nathan Weinstock, **Zionism: False Messiah** (Inklinks, London 1979) page 12.

58. Leon, page 226.

59. Benedict, pages 152-3.

60. There is a good appendix on 'Marx and the Economic-Jew Stereotype' in Draper, volume 1.

61. Leon, page 139.

62. The *conversos* of sixteenth-century Spain, the descendents of Jews who had converted to Christianity, were subjected to persecution despite their Christian faith. This was the time when the Spanish Inquisition against heretics was at its height. The attack on the *conversos* was part of the process of creating a national state in Spain. It would be wrong to reject the racial rather than religious nature of the persecution, but equally wrong to regard it as a precursor of modern racism. Its social and political base was clearly different from the racial anti-semitism of the late nineteenth and early twentieth century. (See Mosse, page xv).

63. The anti-semitism of the movement against aliens developed over time. Jewish Conservative MPs joined the initial clamour for restrictions on

immigration and showed scant sympathy for the poor Jewish immigrants forced to live in the most squalid housing and work in the worst sweatshops.

64. Walvin, **Passage**, page 65.

65. Bernard Gainer, **The Alien Invasion** (Heinemann, London 1972) page 35.

66. Quoted in John A Garrard, **The English and Immigration** (Oxford University Press 1971) page 176.

67. Rollo describes the British Brothers League as 'forerunners of the National Front... one of the first fascist organisations in this country' **(ISJ** 1:96).

68. Gainer, page 70.

69. For instance at a debate in the Toynbee Hall in East London, composed mostly of East End 'working men', not one member of the audience supported a 'West End gentleman' who advocated restriction of 'alien' immigration (Gainer, page 59). Dockers were among those who supported the Jewish tailors' strike of 1889 (Rollo in **ISJ** 1:96).

70. Feeling against the new immigrants was particularly strong in those trades which they commonly entered as sweated labour, such as tailoring, bootmaking and cabinet-making. The argument that the anti-alien movement was a response to the *presence* of 'aliens' is demonstrably false. The British Brothers League was not formed until two decades after the first sizeable immigration of east European Jews. The argument that Britain was incapable of coping with so many new immigrants was equally untrue. In the peak decade of Jewish immigration (1891-1901) there were no more than 60,000 arrivals. Compare this to the more than 300,000 Irish immigrants in the deacde 1841-51.

71. **Labour Leader,** 29 December 1894, quoted in Garrard, page 191 (my emphasis). It is noteworthy that none of Tillet's attacks on 'aliens' was made in the period around 1889, the year of the great dock strike, when the dockers knew exactly who was responsible for their problems.

72. Garrard, page 152.

73. George L Mosse, **International Fascism** (Sage, London 1979) pages 31-2.

74. Daniel Gúerin, **Fascism and Big Business** (Monad, New York 1973) page 80.

75. Guérin, page 79.

76. Robert Benewick, **The Fascist Movement in Britain** (Allen Lane, London 1972) pages 42-7.

77. Soon after the founding of the British Union of Fascists in 1932 Mosley banned anti-semitic activities, but by 1934 he was making it clear that Jews were barred from the movement (Benewick, pages 153-5).

78. See particularly Leon Trotsky, **Fascism: What it is and how to fight it** (Pathfinder, New York 1969); Colin Sparks, **Never Again!** (Bookmarks, London 1980); and Gúerin, **Fascism and Big Business**.

79. Leon, page 236.

80. Leon, page 234.

81. Leon, page 237.

82. Leon, page 238.

83. Leon, page 238.

84. Guérin, page 81.
85. In Britain in the 1980s the fascist groups have tended to use anti-semitism, not for populist appeals, but as part of the process of building a nucleus of hardened and disciplined Nazis.

Chapter 2: RACISM AND IMMIGRATION

1. Walvin, **Black and White**, pages 206-7, and Fryer, pages 298-310.
2. Anthony H Richmond, **The Colour Problem: A Study of Racial Relations** (Penguin, Harmondsworth 1955) pages 240-6. See also Fryer, pages 374-5.
3. Paul Foot, **Immigration and Race in British Politics** (Penguin, Harmondsworth 1965) page 124.
4. See S Joshi and B Carter, 'The Role of Labour in the Creation of a Racist Britain' in **Race and Class**, volume xxv, number 3 (1984) page 56. Senior civil servants would have preferrred 'alien' immigrants, who 'could be removed when no longer required' (Joshi and Carter, page 59), but potential 'alien' immigrants could in general find better conditions elsewhere, for instance in Germany.
5. Walvin, **Passage** 106.
6. Walvin, **Passage** 105. The Resettlement Bill was opposed by Communist MPs Willie Gallacher and Phil Piratin. Gallacher argued that 'The Poles should get coal in their own country' (see Foot, **Immigration**, page 118).
7. Joshi and Carter, page 58 (emphasis added).
8. Joshi and Carter, page 61-4 (emphasis added).
9. See Runnymede Trust and Radical Statistics Race Group, **Britain's Black Population** (Heinemann, London 1980) pages 1-28; Fryer, pages 372-3; and Zig Layton-Henry, 'The New Commonwealth Migrants 1945-62' in **History Today**, December 1985, page 30.
10. Foot, **Immigration**, page 129.
11. **The Spectator**, 4 November 1964, quoted in Foot, **Immigration**, page 129.
12. Cabinet Minutes 39(7), 3 November 1955 (emphasis added).
13. Zig Layton-Henry, **The Politics of Race in Britain** (Allen and Unwin, London 1984) page 32.
14. Cabinet Minutes 39(7), 3 November 1955.
15. By 1961 the total 'coloured' population was 336,600, compared with 415,700 'aliens'. There were also a million Irish people living in Britain, of whom 352,600 had arrived between 1946 and 1959. This latter figure should be compared with an increase of 262,100 in the 'coloured' population in the ten years up to 1961. See Walvin, **Passage**, pages 106 and 111.
16. Layton-Henry, **Politics**, page 25.
17. See also Hugh Gaitskell's argument quoted in Foot, **Immigration**, page 187.
18. Soon after the Notting Hill riot in West London in October 1958, Sir Alec Douglas-Home, then Minister for Commonwealth Relations, said that 'curbs will have be put on the unrestricted flow of immigrants from the West Indies'. That same month the Conservative Party Conference passed a

resolution favouring immigration control. See Layton-Henry, **Politics**, page 36.

19. Ruth Glass, **Newcomers: West Indians in London** (Allen and Unwin, London 1960) page 146.

20. Layton-Henry, **Politics**, page 36.

21. A Sivanandan, **A Different Hunger** (Pluto Press, London 1982) page 105.

22. Foot, **Immigration**, page 163.

23. Foot, **Immigration**, pages 163-9 and 190.

24. Quoted in Layton-Henry, **Politics**, page 53.

25. Foot, **Immigration**, pages 170-1.

26. Foot, **Immigration**, page 173.

27. Quoted in Foot, **Immigration**, page 174.

28. Quoted in Foot, **Immigration**, page 182.

29. Foot, **Immigration**, page 44.

30. Quoted in Foot, **Immigration**, page 59.

31. See Foot, **Immigration**, pages 9-79.

32. Paul Foot, **The Rise of Enoch Powell** (Cornmarket, London 1969), page 73, argues that the events at Smethwick 'drove many Conservatives off the fence and on to the immigration control bandwagon. Among those who made the move was Enoch Powell.'

33. Quoted in Layton-Henry, **Politics**, page 60.

34. Richard Crossman, **Diaries of a Cabinet Minister**, volume 1 (Hamish Hamilton and Jonathan Cape, London 1975) pages 149-50. Crossman later reflected on the change in Labour's immigration policy: '...I am convinced that if we hadn't done all this we would have been faced with certain electoral defeat in the West Midlands and the South East. Politically, fear of immigration is the most powerful undertow today. Moreover, we had already abandonned the Gaitskell position when we renewed the Immigration Act (of 1962), and any attempt now to resist demands for reduced quotas would have been fatal. We felt we had to out-trump the Tories by doing what they would have done and so transforming their policy into a bi-partisan policy. I fear we were right; and partly I think so because I am an old-fashioned Zionist who believes that anti-Semitism and racialism are endemic, that one has to deal with them by controlling immigration when it gets beyond a certain level (**Diaries**, page 299). Crossman told a West Midlands rally: 'Two years ago the Conservatives instituted completely ineffective controls and now they blame us because the flood of illegal immigrants is threatening to undermine the efforts which local authorites are making' (quoted in Foot, **Immigration**, page 183).

35. Foot, **Immigration**, page 193.

36. Robert Moore, **Racism and Black Resistance in Britain** (Pluto Press, London 1975) pages 25 and 27. Later, when in opposition in 1972, the Labour Party produced a Green Paper which argued that a discriminatory policy on immigration made integration more difficult and contributed to racial hostility (see Layton-Henry, **Politics**, page 84).

37. Foot, **Powell**, page 110. Foot shows that only 120,000 British Asians

from Kenya could claim a right of entry. Powell had inflated the figures. When Powell whipped up racist fears in 1968, the first response of James Callaghan, then Home Secretary, was to state that the Labour government had been deporting immigrants for two years (Robert Moore, 'Labour and Colour 1945-68' in **Venture**, September 1968).

38. This was even more than the Tories were demanding. They had argued for a phased entry of the Kenyan Asians (**Britain' Black Population,** page 33).

39. **Britain's Black Population**, page 33. Also naturalisation and registration in the UK as a citizen of the UK and Colonies, or adoption in the UK.

40. Quoted by Moore, in **Venture**.

41. This was accepted by the Labour Party's own **1978 Campaign Handbook**, page 2, which declared: 'Labour will repeal the 1968 and 1971 Immigration Acts to eliminate the racialist concepts of patriality'. By 1978 Labour had already had four years in government in which to repeal the old legislation, and had not done so.

42. Richard Crossman, **Diaries of a Cabinet Minister**, volume 2 (Hamish Hamilton and Jonathan Cape, London 1977) page 679.

43. Crossman, volume 2, page 679.

44. Quoted in Layton-Henry, **Politics**, page 71.

45. Foot, **Powell**, page 116.

46. Martin Kettle and Lucy Hodges, **Uprising!** (Pan, London 1982) page 52.

47. Walvin, **Passage** 172

48. Foot, **Powell**, page 111.

49. **1978 Campaign Handbook**, page 58.

50. 'Weekend World', 4 February 1978, quoted in **The Case against Immigration Controls** (Socialist Workers Party, London 1978).

51. Layton-Henry, **Politics**, page 99.

52. Following the first murder, Kingsley Read of the National Party declared: 'One down, one million to go'. When Read was acquitted of a charge of incitement to racial hatred, the judge told him: 'By all means propagate the view you hold. I wish you well.' (Kettle and Hodges, page 60).

53. **Labour's Programme 1983** (Labour Party, London 1982) pages 191-3.

54. See Peter Alexander, 'Racism: A parliamentary pawn' in **Socialist Review**, number 52 (March 1983), page 14.

55. **The Guardian**. 5 July 1986.

56. Quoted in **Socialist Worker**, 28 July 1986.

57. See **Daily Mirror**, 9 June 1986.

58. **Labour's Programme 1982**, page 192. See also page 273 on refugees. Given that Labour expects 'no more than 1000 a year' extra immigrants, there will be difficulty in fulfilling its commitment to dependents.

59. **Immigration Policy Statement** (Labour Party, London 1982).

60. Quoted in Foot, **Immigration**, page 187.

61. Vishnu Sharma, **No Racist Immigration Laws** (Communist Party, London 1979) pages 15-16.

Chapter 3: RACISM TODAY

1. Interviewed by David Frost, 3 January 1969, quoted in Martin Barker, **The New Racism** (Junction Books, London 1981) page 40.
2. Quoted in Barker, page 39.
3. Quoted in Barker, page 15.
4. See chapter 2, note 15.
5. Fryer, page 374.
6. **British Social Attitudes** (HMSO, London 1986) page 125.
7. **Gallup International Public Opinion Polls: Great Britain 1937-75**, volume 1, page 478, and **British Social Attitudes**, pages 126-7.
8. Quoted in E J B Rose and others, **Colour and Citizenship** (Oxford University Press 1969).
9. **British Social Attitudes**, page 129.
10. Colin Brown, **Black and White in Britain: The Third Policy Studies Institute Report** (Gower, London 1985) page 286, reports that 50 per cent agreed with the view that 'The present laws against discrimination should be enforced more effectively'. Only 31 per cent disagreed.
11. The one important exception has been the decline in the proportion of people opposing immigration controls. Those in favour of allowing free entry to Britain fell from 37 per cent in 1958 to only 1 per cent ten years later, while those in favour of controls rose from 53 per cent to 95 per cent (Rose, page 594).
12. Fryer, page 374.
13. **Gallup**, page 478.
14. Fryer, page 376. The most notable examples were disputes involving busworkers in Wolverhampton and West Bromwich in 1955.
15. David J Smith, **Racial Disadvantage in Britain** (Penguin, Harmondsworth 1977). The fieldwork for this report was conducted in the second half of 1974, when 18 per cent of workers had experienced stoppages at work within the past year.
16. Foot, **Immigration**, page 127.
17. The 1965 Act outlawed discrimination in public places. The 1968 Act extended its provisions to include discrimination in employment and housing. The 1976 Act included indirect discrimination and made it illegal to encourage racial hatred.
18. Foot, **Powell**, page 102.
19. For instance the 1976 Act was used against the fascist groups only after they had been defeated in 1979.
20. Paul Gordon, **White Law: Racism in the police, courts and prisons** (Pluto, London 1983) page 17.
21. **Britain's Black Population**, page 39.
22. The issue of whether or not to participate in the government's race relations machinery was a major factor in splitting both the Campaign against Racial Discrimination and the Indian Workers Association.
23. Sivanandan, page 118.
24. Ann Dummett, **A Portrait of English Racism** (CARAF, London 1984)

page 131.

25. Moore, **Racism**, page 16, makes the following important point: 'Migrants are here because our rulers created the conditions in their homelands which made migration necessary, as well as a situation in Europe into which migration was possible.'

26. Smith, page 75.

27. The following table is taken from Brown, page 223:

Job levels of whites, Asians and West Indians in 1974 and 1982 (column percentages)

Men	White		West Indian		Asian	
	1974	1982	1974	1982	1974	1982
Professional, Employer, Manager	23	22	2	7	7	14
Other non-manual	17	20	6	9	11	12
Skilled Manual and Foreman	42	44	59	48	40	36
Semi-skilled Manual	12	11	23	23	30	31
Unskilled Manual	6	3	9	11	11	5

Women	White		West Indian		Asian	
	1975/6	1982	1974	1982	1974	1982
Professional, Employer, Manager	5	9	1	1	2	7
Other non-manual	51	52	42	53	30	35
Skilled Manual and Foreman	7	9	8	3	13	14
Semi-skilled manual	36	19	41	36	47	42
Unskilled Manual		11	6	6	8	3

Notes: (1) Figures for white women in 1975/6 derived from General Household Survey (Table 5.9, **Social Trends** No 8, 1975)
(2) Bases for the 1974 survey include all people in the job market who have worked, whether employed or self-employed.
(3) Bases for the 1982 survey include only those in work, whether employed or self-employed.
(4) White figures are for all areas (nationally representative).

28. Brown, page 226.
29. Brown, page 147.
30. Brown, page 127.
31. Brown, page 127.
32. Anne Newnham, **Employment, Unemployment and Black People** (Runnymede 1986), pages 11 and 17. The **Labour Force Survey 1984** (HMSO 1984) gives the following figures:

Unemployment rates by ethnic origin and sex, 1984 (percentages)

	men	women	both sexes
All	11.5	10.5	11.1
White	11.0	10.1	10.6
Non-White	21.3	19.1	20.4

of which:

West Indian and Guyanese	29	17	23.0
Indian	13	18	15.2
Pakistani and Bangladeshi	34	40	34.6

Unemployment among 16-24 year olds, 1984 (percentages)

	men	women
White	19	16
Afro-Caribbean	41	26
Asian	26	35

33. Using information provided by the unemployed about their previous jobs, Brown was able to calculate what the unemployment rates for Whites would be if their job levels were the same as those of black workers. The White unemployment rate for men would then be about 17 per cent if job levels were the same as those of Asians, 19 per cent if the same as West Indians. These hypothetical rates were not as high as those actually found among Asians and West Indians (20 and 25 per cent respectively), but they were much higher than the actual rate among Whites at the time of the survey (13 per cent). See Brown, page 154.

34. The unemployment rates for men in inner city areas of London, Birmingham and Manchester were 23 per cent for Whites, 29 per cent for West Indians and 26 per cent for Asians - proportionally much more similar than those for Britain as a whole. However, only 6 per cent of the country's White population lives in these areas, compared with 41 per cent of West Indians and 23 per cent of Asians. (Brown, page 192).

35. Colin Brown and Pat Gay, **Racial Discrimination: Seventeen years after the Act** (Policy Studies Institute, London 1985).

36. **The Guardian**, 27 November 1985. See Newnham, page 25.

37. Banton, page 50.

38. Snowden, **Before Colour Prejudice**, page 67.

Chapter 4: THE RISE OF BLACK RESISTANCE

1. I intend to concentrate on the high points of Black-led struggles in the United States. A number of other movements, organisations and individuals have played an important part in the history of Black America, among them the Populist Movement, the Knights of Labor, the IWW, Booker T Washington, W E B DuBois, the NAACP and the CIO. An excellent series of articles on these was published in **Socialist Worker** (Chicago) during 1985-6.

2. Len Silva, 'The Real History of Slavery's End' in **Socialist Worker** (Chicago) February 1985.

3. Nancy Maclean, 'Reconstruction in the post-Civil War South' in **Socialist Worker** (Chicago) March 1985, and 'The Promise and Failure of Populism' in **Socialist Worker** (Chicago) April 1985.

4. Theodore C Vincent, **Black Power and the Garvey Movement** (Ramparts, San Francisco 1971) page 134.

5. Robert Bagnall quoted in E David Cronon, **Black Moses: The Story of**

Marcus Garvey (University of Wisconsin Press 1969) page 107.

6. Quoted in Adolph Edwards, **Marcus Garvey** (New Beacon, London 1967) page 9.

7. C L R James, **A History of Negro Revolt** (Race Today, London 1985) page 52.

8. Harry Haywood, **Black Bolshevik: Autobiography of an Afro-American Communist** (Liberator, Chicago 1978) page 102.

9. Vincent, page 127.

10. Cronon, pages 62-4.

11. Emory J Tolbert, **The UNIA and Black Los Angeles** (Center for Afro-American Studies, Los Angeles 1980) page 3.

12. Cronon, page 49.

13. According to Philip Foner, **Organised Labor and the Black Worker 1619-1973** (International Publishers, New York 1974) page 144: 'By 1919 there were four million workers... striking for higher wages.'

14. William Foster, **The Negro People in American History** (International, New York 1954) page 440.

15. Philip Foner, **American Socialism and Black Americans** (Greenwood, Connecticut 1977) page 291.

16. Foster, page 441. He claims that these figures underestimate the actual losses. At the time of the riot workers in the slaughterhouses, black and white, were flocking into the unions in expectation of a strike. Foster, who was himself the key union organiser involved, claims that the Chicago riot was instigated by agents of the slaughterhouse bosses.

17. August 1920. Quoted in Tolbert, page 11.

18. November 1919. Quoted in Vincent, page 43.

19. Leon Trotsky, **On Black Nationalism and Self-determination** (Pathfinder, New York 1967) page 46.

20. Quoted in Haywood, page 125.

21. This riot ended with dynamite bombs being dropped by airplane on to black neighbourhoods. See Vincent, page 75.

22. Lee Sustar, 'The African Blood Brotherhood' in **Socialist Worker** (Chicago) September 1985.

23. Vincent, page 76.

24. James, **Negro Revolt**, page 53.

25. The NAACP was founded in 1909. Its leading spokesman in its early years was W E B DuBois. Although led by Blacks, it has always included a substantial white membership. Today it tends to work with the Democratic Party.

26. Cronon, page 75.

27. Cronon, page 200.

28. Quoted in Cronon, page 198.

29. Cronon, page 190.

30. Cronon, page 196.

31. C L R James, 'The Revolutionary Answer to the Negro Problem (1948)' in **The Future in the Present** (Allison and Busby, London 1977).

32. Christina Baker, 'The politics of Marcus Garvey' in **Socialist Worker**

(Chicago) July 1985.

33. **The Second Congress of the Communist International: Minutes of the Proceedings,** in two volumes (London 1977) page 124.

34. Foster, page 463.

35. Trotsky, **On Black Nationalism,** page 14.

36. Trotsky, **On Black Nationalism,** pages 20-31. The discussion took place in Prinkipo, Turkey, in 1933.

37. Trotsky, **On Black Nationalism,** pages 38-49. Discussion held in Coyoacan, Mexico, in 1939.

38. Mark Naison, **Communists in Harlem during the Depression** (Grove, New York 1984) page 18.

39. Naison, page 134.

40. Naison, page 47.

41. Naison, page 47.

42. Naison, page 150.

43. Naison, page 229.

44. Naison, page 280. At least two-thirds of these black members were in Harlem.

45. Naison, page 185.

46. Naison, pages 269-70.

47. Naison, page 264.

48. Quoted in Naison, page 256.

49. Naison, page 273.

50. Lee Suster, 'The Montgomery Bus Boycott' in **Socialist Worker** (Chicago) November 1986.

51. Bureau of the Census, **The Social and Economic Status of the Black Population in the United States,** quoted in Manning Marable, **How Capitalism underdeveloped Black America** (Pluto Press, London 1983) page 310.

52. Martin Luther King, **Strike towards Freedom** (Harper and Row, New York 1958) page 46.

53. In particular the students played an important part in preparing less-educated black people for the tests which had to be passed before they were allowed to register as voters.

54. Manning Marable, **Black American Politics** (Verso, London 1985) page 92.

55. Ian Taylor, 'Malcolm X' in **Socialist Worker** (London), 9 November 1985.

56. Marable, **Black American,** page 96. Johnson was then president, Kennedy having been assassinated.

57. Marable, **Black American,** page 90. The protests were also taking off in the North. Foner, **Organised Labor,** page 346, notes that between May and 15 August 1963 there were 978 demonstrations in 209 cities or towns in 36 states.

58. James A Geschwender, **Class, Race and Worker Insurgency** (Cambridge University Press 1977) page 71.

59. Marable, **How Capitalism,** page 208.

60. Bureau of the Census.

61. Kim Moody, 'The American Working Class in Transition' in **ISJ** 1:40

(October-November 1969) page 18.

62. Geschwender, page 70.
63. Moody, page 18.
64. Bureau of the Census.
65. From the McCone Commission Report, cited in Della Rossa, **Why Watts Exploded** (Merit, New York 1966) page 14.
66. Foner, **Organised Labor**, page 358.
67. Della Rossa, page 13.
68. Cited by Chris Harman, 'The Summer of '81' in **ISJ** 2:14 (Autumn 1981).
69. Geschwender, page 72.
70. Foner, **Organised Labor**, page 356.
71. Della Rossa, page 11. According to **The Black Uprisings** (Merit, New York 1967), Martin Luther King, A Philip Randolph and Ray Wilkins (NAACP) issued a statement condemning the rebellions as 'criminal' acts. Another black leader, Bayard Rustin, who had led the March on Washington, justified 'whatever force is necessary' to stop rioting, because 'if the rioting continues, an atmosphere will be created in which established civil rights leadership will be robbed of standing'.
72. Foner, **Organised Labor**, page 40.
73. Della Rossa, page 19.
74. Stokely Carmichael and Charles V Hamilton, **Black Power** (Penguin, Harmondsworth 1967) page 22.
75. Eugene D Genovese, **In Red and Black** (Vintage, New York 1968) page 239.
76. In reality these are traditions within petty bourgeois politics. We will consider some of the experience of working-class politics in the final chapter.
77. Malcolm X, **Autobiography** (Penguin, Harmondsworth 1965) page 397.
78. George Breitman, **The Last Year of Malcolm X** (Pathfinder, New York 1967) page 10.
79. Malcolm X, page 424.
80. Malcolm X, page 421.
81. It is possible that Malcolm X was assassinated by a supporter of the Nation of Islam.
82. Malcolm X, pages 479 and 494-6.
83. Malcolm X, page 489.
84. Breitman, page 33.
85. Breitman, page 39.
86. Sivanandan.
87. Eldridge Cleaver, **Post-Prison Writings and Speeches** (Panther, London 1971) page 56.
88. Cleaver, page 177.
89. Bobby Seale, **Seize the Time** (Arrow, London 1970) page 473.
90. Huey P Newton, **Revolutionary Suicide** (Wildwood House, New York 1973) page 116.
91. Laurie and Sy Landy, 'The Black Panther Party Splits' in **ISJ** 1:48 (June-July 1971) page 6.

92. Seale, page 432.

93. Newton, page 329.

94. Dan Georgakas and Martin Surkin, **Detroit: I do mind dying** (St Martins Press, New York 1975) page 155.

95. Landy and Landy, page 6.

96. Newton, page 331.

97. Foner, **Organised Labor**, pages 401-20.

98. Extrapolation from figures provided by Geschwender, page 59.

99. Geschwender, page 42-4.

100. Foner, **Organised Labor**, page 411.

101. Georgakas and Surkin, page 33. In 1969 the average Black wage for experienced workers in the auto industry was 85.3 per cent of that paid to Whites. In the South Blacks received only 76.3 per cent of the comparable white wage. See Geschwender, page 46.

102. Foner, **Organised Labor**, page 410.

103. Foner, **Organised Labor**, page 406.

104. Georgakas and Surkin, pages 53-62.

105. Geschwender, page 184.

106. Georgakas and Surkin, page 63.

107. Quoted in Geschwender, page 138.

108. Quoted in Georgakas and Surkin, page 20.

109. Quoted in Georgakas and Surkin, page 71.

110. Georgakas and Surkin, pages 46-8; Foner, **Organised Labor**, page 414. Geschwender, page s 92-3, says the wildcat lasted three days. There are other minor factual differences between the accounts.

111. Fred Pilgotsky, 'US: Workers on the move' in **ISJ** 1:70 (June 1974).

112. Foner, **Organised Labor**, page 417.

113. Even before DRUM was formed, Local 3, for instance, had a black president.

114. Geschwender, page 185.

115. Georgakas and Surkin, page 163.

116. Quoted in Geschwender, page 178.

117. Georgakas and Surkin, page 168.

118. Pilgotsky, page 27.

119. Georgakas and Surkin, page 39.

120. Georgakas and Surkin, page 111.

121. Geschwender, page 179, quotes Mike Hamlin in full: 'From the beginning at Dodge we wrote off any possible mobilisation of white workers during that period. That is not to say that some of us did not understand that the working class is multi-national and that there has to be unity of the entire working class. But during that time, we deliberately and consciously wrote off white workers.'

Chapter 5: THE DECLINE OF BLACK RESISTANCE

1. Marable, **Black American**, pages 262-4.

2. Quoted by Manning Marable, 'In the Business of Prophet-making' in

New Statesman, 13 December 1985.

3.   Marable, **Black American**, page 173.
4.   Marable, **Black American**, pages 97-8; Marable, **How Capitalism**, page 103; and Bureau of the Census (1980) table 125.
5.   There was also some expansion of black businesses, but they have been increasingly squeezed by the recession. Marable comments caustically that all the major Black-run companies combined could be purchased by Mobil Oil just using its liquid assets.
6.   Marable in **New Statesman**, 13 December 1985.
7.   Marable, **Black American**, pages 191-247.
8.   Marable, **Black American**, page 244.
9.   **Socialist Worker** (Chicago), June 1985, page 3.
10. Marable, **How Capitalism**, page 38.
11. Foner, **Organised Labor**, page 425.
12. Marable, **Black American**, page 41.
13. Among Rastafarians Garvey has the status of a prophet because he predicted the coming of a black emperor to rule an African nation. The sect itself emerged from the ranks of the Jamaican UNIA in the 1930s. It takes its name from Ras (or King) Tafari, Haile Selassie's Ethiopian name. When Selassie was in London in 1935 he made it clear that he did not desire contact with black men. Garvey, also living in London, attacked him as 'the ruler of a country where black men are chained and flogged' (Cronon, page 162).
14. **Socialist Worker** (London), 7 March and 11 April 1981. These were two of the largest mobilisations of black people ever in Britain.
15. Quoted in Harman, **ISJ** 2:14, page 12. This is by far the best analysis of the riots, but there is also useful material in Kettle and Hodges.
16. Harman in **ISJ** 2:14, page 13. Georgakas and Surkin, page 187, suggest that the Whites were mostly poor Whites from the Appalachians.
17. Harman in **ISJ** 2:14, page 14.
18. **British Social Attitudes**, page 98.
19. Brown, page 171.
20. Brown, page 282.
21. William Brink and Louis Harris, (Simon and Schuster, New York 1966) page 234.

Chapter 6: RACISM AND REFORMISM

1.   J H Winter, 'The Webbs and the non-white world: a case of socialist realism' in **Journal of Contemporary History**, volume ix (January 1974) page 185.
2.   Quoted in Winter, page 189.
3.   Quoted in Winter, page 191.
4.   Winter, page 192.
5.   **Labour Leader**, 2 July 1905 (published by the Independent Labour Party).
6.   **Clarion**, 15 and 22 October 1892, quoted in David Howell, **British Workers and the Independent Labour Party 1888-1906** (Manchester University

Press 1983) page 384.

Labour Leader, 30 March 1904.

8. Among the opponents of the 1919 Act was Clement Attlee, who argued that 'these Aliens Restriction Acts are thoroughly bad Acts... they are inspired by a sort of crude nationalism'. This did not prevent Attlee and three other Labour prime ministers implementing the Act. (See Foot, **Immigration**, page 112).

9. Foot, **Immigration**, page 113.

10. Foot, **Immigration**, page 113.

11. Foot, **Immigration**, page 114.

12. Foot, **Immigration**, page 113.

13. Quoted in **Socialist Worker** (London), 27 July 1985.

14. Quoted in **Socialist Worker** (London), 27 July 1985.

15. Quoted in Colin Sparks, 'Labour and Imperialism', in **ISJ** 2:26 (Spring 1985) page 56.

16. Sparks, in **ISJ** 2:26, page 59.

17. Sparks, in **ISJ** 2:26, page 62.

18. John Newsinger, 'Revolt in the Empire' in **Socialist Worker Review**, number 76 (May 1985) page 36.

19. Alex Callinicos, 'The Respectable Renegade' in **Socialist Worker Review**, number 79 (September 1985) quoting Ben Pimlott, **Hugh Dalton** (Jonathan Cape, London 1985).

20. Quoted in Foot, **Immigration**, page 53.

21. **The Guardian**, 1 October 1985.

22. Quoted in Sparks, in **ISJ** 2:26, page 54.

23. Cabinet Minutes 39(7), 3 November 1955, and Cabinet Papers (55)166.

24. **Black People and the Criminal Justice System** (NACRO, London 1986).

25. Brown, page 276. Similarly a Harris Poll conducted for ITV's 'Weekend World' just after the Tottenham riot showed that two-thirds of Blacks considered that the police discriminated against them (**Daily Express**, 14 October 1985).

26. Gordon, page 65.

27. Runnymede Trust, **Race and Immigration**, number 196 (October 1986) page 8.

28. Policy Studies Institute.

29. Quoted in **The Times** and **The Standard**, 8 October 1985; **The Times**, 9 October 1985.

30. **News of the World** and **Sunday Mirror**, 13 October 1985.

31. See particularly two books by Paul Gordon of the Runnymede Trust: **White Law** and **Policing Immigration: Britain's Internal Control** (Pluto Press, London 1985).

32. See particularly Joe Sim, 'Scarman: The police counter-attack' in **Socialist Register 1982** (Merlin, London 1982).

33. Gareth Pierce in **The Guardian**, 15 March 1982.

34. For instance the Policy Studies Institute report **Police and People in London** found that 70 per cent of West Indians in vehicles were stopped and searched without sufficient reason, compared with 49 per cent of Whites and

29 per cent of Asians. Of those on foot 66 per cent of West Indians were stopped without sufficient reason compared to 32 per cent of Whites and 23 per cent of Asians. The **Islington Crime Survey** (1986) showed that black people were twice as likely to be stopped as Whites. In the previous year 53 per cent of young Blacks in Islington had been stopped by the police.

35. Gordon, **White Law**, page 71.
36. Gordon, **White Law**, page 72.
37. Quoted in **The Guardian**, 15 June 1985.
38. Quoted in **The Guardian**, 21 September 1985.
39. Quoted in **Socialist Worker**, 15 November 1985.
40. **The Standard**, 8 October 1985.
41. **The Guardian**, 14 October 1985.
42. **Daily Telegraph**, 14 October 1985.
43. **Black Sections Newsletter**, Spring 1986.
44. Tony Cliff and Donny Gluckstein, **Marxism and Trade Union Struggle** (Bookmarks, London 1986) page 269.
45. Gainer, page 157.
46. David Coates, **The Labour Party and the Struggle for Socialism** (Cambridge 1976) page 137.
47. **New Statesman**, 17 January 1986, page 16.
48. Quoted in Barker, page 38.
49. Actually the proposal came from a shop steward in the Communist Party, but their approach has much in common with the dominant attitudes in the Labour Party.
50. Maggie Falshaw, 'Course for a Change?' in **Socialist Worker Review**, number 85 (March 1986); also Paul Ahmed, 'Changing course', in **Socialist Worker Review**, number 84 (February 1986).
51. Eamonn McCann, **War and an Irish Town** (Penguin, Harmondsworth 1974).

Chapter 7: THE REVOLUTIONARY SOCIALIST ALTERNATIVE

1. Letter from Marx to Weydemeyer, 1852, quoted in Hal Draper, **Karl Marx's Theory of Revolution**, volume 3 (Monthly Review, New York 1986), page 247. Marx's own italics.
2. Draper, volume 2, page 66.
3. Karl Marx and Friedrich Engels, **Manifesto of the Communist Party** (Peking 1973) page 44.
4. **Manifesto**, page 48.
5. **Manifesto**, page 46.
6. A Szymanski, 'Racial discrimination and White gain', in **American Sociological Review**, 41:3 (1976) page 405.
7. Szymanski, pages 409-410.
8. Szymanski, page 411.
9. Szymanski, page 412.
10. It is sometimes suggested that *all* Whites, as opposed to a white ruling class, benefitted from the racism of imperialism. This is refuted by Tony Cliff

in 'The economic roots of reformism', in **Neither Washington nor Moscow** (Bookmarks, London 1982) pages 108-117.

11. Antonio Gramsci, **Selections from Prison Notebooks** (Lawrence and Wishart, London 1971) pages 324 and 333.

12. John Molyneux, **The Future Socialist Society** (Socialist Workers Party, London 1987) page 31,

13. The International Working Men's Association is also known as the First International. John Molyneux argues that the IWMA 'created a much more widespread awareness of at least some of Marx's basic principles than had ever existed before. Above all, it established the tradition of international organisation at the heart of the working-class socialist movement. These were great achievements...' (John Molyneux, **Marxism and the Party** (Bookmarks, London 1986) page 49).

14. The names of Davidson and Wedderburn appear on the list of '33 leading reformers' which the police prepared for the Home Secretary in 1819. Davidson was eventually hanged and decapitated for his part in the Cato Street Conspiracy. There are good accounts of the black radicals in Fryer and in Ron Ramdin, **The Making of the Black Working Class in Britain** (Gower, London 1987).

15. Fryer, page 225, quoting the report of a police informer.

16. Fryer, page 223. Fryer's emphasis.

17. Fryer, page 239.

18. Fryer, page 244.

19. Quoted in Frederick Engels, 'Feargus O'Connor and the Irish People' (1848), in Marx and Engels, **Articles on Britain** (Progress, Moscow 1975) page 75. O'Connor impressed Engels because he spoke 'not only as an Irishman but also, and primarily, as an English democrat and as a Chartist.'

20. David Milton, **The Politics of US Labor** (Monthly Review, New York 1982) page 89.

21. Daniel Guérin, **100 Years of Labor in the USA** (Inklinks, London 1979) page 150.

22. Foner, **Organised Labor**, pages 229-30.

23. Foner, **Organised Labor**, page 216.

24. Foner, **Organised Labor**, page 224.

25. Quoted in Foner, **Organised Labor**, page 232.

26. Quoted in Foner, **Organised Labor**, page 237.

27. Guérin, **100 Years**, page 158.

28. V I Lenin, **What is to be done?** (Peking, 1973) page 104.

29. Lenin, **What is to be done?**, page 98.

30. Lenin, **What is to be done?**, page 99.

31. V I Lenin, **Collected Works**, volume 22 (Moscow) pages 355-7.

32. V I Lenin, 'The Position of the Bund within the Party' (1903), in Hyman Lumar (editor) **Lenin on the Jewish Question** (International Publishers, New York 1974) page 48.

33. V I Lenin, 'The Nationality of Pupils in Russian Schools' (1913), in **Lenin on the Jewish Question**, page 93. On the following page Lenin adds: '...under real democracy it is quite possible to ensure instruction in the native

language, in native history and so forth, *without* splitting up the schools according to nationality.'

34. V I Lenin, 'Once more on the Segregation of the Schools according to Nationality' (1913) in **Lenin on the Jewish Question**, pages 98-9. Here he makes the point that 'The right of a nation to use its native language is explicitly and definitely recognised in the Marxist programme.'

35. For details, see **Lenin on the Jewish Question**, page 139. Among those impressed by the Bolsheviks' commitment to national self-determination was Marcus Garvey, who sent a message of solidarity to the Russian leaders.

36. **Lenin on the Jewish Question**, page 142.

37. **Lenin on the Jewish Question**, pages 14-15.

38. Weinstock, pages 22-3.

39. Quoted in Nigel Harris, **Beliefs in Society** (Penguin, Harmondsworth 1971) page 162.

40. Harris, page 159.

41. Quoted in Mike Simons, 'Whose fortress now?', in **Socialist Worker Review**, number 79 (September 1985).

Index

(Britain): 40
Griffiths, Peter: 35-6
Grunwicks strike (Britain):
Guerin, Daniel: 26, 28, 143

Haile Selassie: 100
Hain, Peter: 154
Hamlin, Mike: 88, 92-4
Hardie, J Keir: 44, 145
Haringey Council (London): 118, 124, 126, 148
Harlem District (New York): 60, 66-70, 97
Harman, Chris: 105
Harris, Nigel: 151-2
Hattersley, Roy: 36, 43, 50, 116, 118, 121-2
Hawkins, John: 7
Healey, Denis: 35
Heath, Edward: 38
Heffer, Eric: 122
Hendon Police College (London): 120
Hitler, Adolf: 16-17, 26, 97, 148
Hitler-Stalin Pact (1939): 69
Holborow, Paul: 155
Hong Kong: 41
Housing: 1, 31, 33-4, 43, 47, 52, 55, 129
Howe, Geoffrey: 50
Hume, David: 8

Idrish, Mohammed: 156
Immigration (into Britain):
—Asian: 17
—Irish: 17-20, 30-1,
—Jewish: 22-4, 46
—Kenyan: 37
—Malawian: 39
—Pakistani: 36
—Polish: 30
—West Indian: 17, 31
Immigration Act (Britain, 1971): 38-9, 41
Immigration controls: 24, 41-2, 114, 117, 152-3, 158
Immigration officers: 1, 40, 117, 120-1
Immigration Service Union (Britain): 117
Imperialism: 11, 14-15, 19, 115-117, 152
India: 6, 16, 31, 115
Indian Workers Association (Britain): 104
Industrial Revolution: 18

Industrial Workers of the World (IWW): 60, 64, 142
Inner city problems: 33-4, 52, 104
Integration: 78
Internationalism: 138, 150-1
Ireland: 17-18, 129, 141
Isaacs, George: 30
Islington Council (London): 125, 157

Jackson, Jesse: 2, 71, 96-7, 148
Jackson, Maynard: 100
James, C L R: 5, 8, 62, 64
Jarret, Cynthia: 118, 120
Jews: 20-6, 55, 113, 148-151
'Jim Crow' Laws: 59, 70-3
Johnson, Lyndon: 73-4
Jones, LeRoi (Baraka, Amiri): 96

Kaufman, Gerald: 41
Keith, Sir Arthur: 15
Kennedy, John F: 73-4
Kenya: 115
Khama, Seretse: 116
King, Martin Luther: 71, 73-4, 77, 97, 100
Kingsley, Charles: 17-18
Kinnock, Neil: 42, 109, 116, 118, 120-2, 127
Kipling, Rudyard: 13
Knights of Labor (USA): 64, 142
Ku Klux Klan (USA): 59, 63, 72
Knox, Robert: 16

Labour market: 20-1, 30, 32-4, 39, 42-3, 51-2
Labour Party (Britain): 2, 30, 32, 34-41, 50, 107-9, 112-131, 145, 154-5, 157-8
—Black Sections: 2, 109-110, 112, 116, 121-6, 128-9
—electoralism: 2, 36, 40, 118, 122-3, 125-6, 139
—Labour-controlled councils: 121, 123-4
—1978 Campaign Handbook: 37, 39
—1982 Programme: 41
League of Revolutionary Black Workers (USA): 88, 93-4, 102
Leese, Arnold: 26
Lenin, V I: 64, 89, 145-151
Leon, Abram: 20-3, 27
Lewis, John L: 142-3
Lewisham anti-racist demonstration

Other publications

Arguments for Revolutionary Socialism
by John Molyneux

Aims to answer all the questions and objections to socialism: 'You can't change human nature', 'Do you call Russia socialist?', 'Don't revolutions mean violence?', 'You socialists would abolish democracy'. In answering these, this book sets out socialist arguments in a way that can contribute to everyday discussion, and shows how the many and various arguments for revolutionary socialism are but parts of one argument, one analysis: of how the world we live in works, and how socialists can change it. £2.50 / US$4.75

The Future Socialist Society
by John Molyneux

What will life be like in a socialist society? How would socialism solve, for instance, the world food crisis? Will the socialist revolution really emancipate women? This pamphlet draws on the basic ideas of Marxism and the experience of workers' revolutions of the past century to show the vision of socialism. 95p / US$1.75

Russia: From workers' state to state capitalism
by Chris Harman

If the vision of a future socialist society is to offer any hope for a world in crisis today, then some tough questions must be answered:

What happened after the Russian workers' revolution of October 1917?

What brought to power the bureaucracy headed by Stalin?

Is Russia socialist, as its rulers would have us believe?

Is such dictatorship the inevitable result of workers' revolution—as our own rulers would have us believe?

To these hard questions, this book offers hard answers. £2.50 / US$4.75

Bailing out the System
Reformist socialism in Western Europe 1944-1985
by Ian Birchall

In 1945 an astute Tory politician told the House of Commons: 'If you do not give the people reform, they are going to give you revolution.' In the years since then, reformism has again and again saved the capitalist system from disaster, defusing working-class struggle whenever it threatened to bring radical change. This book shows how. £5.95 / US$12.00

These and many more publications are available from bookshops and local branches of the socialist organisations listed at the front of this book, or by post from:

Bookmarks, 265 Seven Sisters Road, London N4 2DE, England
Bookmarks, PO Box 16085, Chicago, IL 60616, USA
Bookmarks, GPO Box 1473N, Melbourne 3001, Australia